APPLE WATCH

SERIES 9

USER GUIDE

The Complete Practical Step By Step User Manual To Help Beginners And Seniors To Demystify & Master The New Apple Watch Series 9. With WatchOS Tips & Tricks

By

Tech Titans

Copyright © 2023 Tech Titans

Table of Contents

INTRODUCTION

New features and a major step forward for the environment are part of Apple's next iteration of the Apple Watch, Series 9. Improved performance and functionality are provided by the new S9 SiP in Apple Watch Series 9. Other enhancements include a quicker on-device version of Siri with access to and logging of health data, a brighter display, Precision Finding for iPhone, and a novel double-tap gesture. The Series 9 Apple Watch is powered by watchOS 10, which brings updated applications, a revamped Smart Stack, fresh watch faces, enhanced cycling and hiking capabilities, and mental health tracking and management functions.

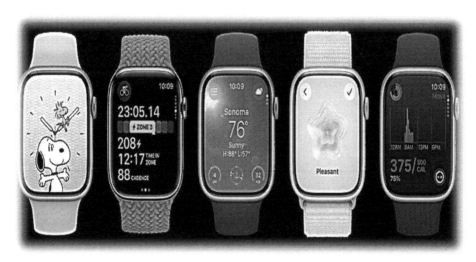

Apple's ambition to be carbon neutral throughout its entire company, manufacturing supply chain, and product life cycle by 2030 has reached a major milestone with the introduction of a carbon neutral option for every Apple Watch.

The new Apple Watch collection is now available for preorder, and will begin shipping on September 22.

CHAPTER ONE

FEATURES OF APPLE WATCH SERIES 9

According to Apple COO Jeff Williams, "Apple Watch is an indispensable companion that helps millions of people with their health, fitness, communications, and safety." "We're presenting our most advanced Apple Watch family yet, packed with features like a new double-tap gesture, brighter display, on-device Siri, and our first-ever carbon neutral goods. Whether it's an upgrade from an older model or a first Apple Watch, the time is now to get involved.

This year, Apple reached a significant benchmark on the path to its Apple 2030 target, according to Lisa Jackson, Apple's vice president of Environment, Policy, and Social Initiatives. According to Apple, "our first carbon neutral products were made in a uniquely Apple way, steeply reducing carbon emissions from materials, electricity, and transportation through innovation and design."

In front of a white background are four carbon-neutral Apple Watch Series 9 models.

Apple's first carbon neutral goods are Apple Watch Series 9 models with certain casing and band configurations.

The New S9 Sip

The S9 SiP, exclusive to the Apple Watch Series 9, is a custom-designed piece of Apple silicon. Apple's most advanced watch processor to date brings a host of system-wide enhancements and new capabilities, including as a double-tap gesture and an in-watch version of Siri with safe and private health data access and logging. The new 4-core Neural Engine in the Apple Watch Series 9 is capable of doing machine learning tasks at double the speed of the previous generation. Apple Watch Series 9 has an 19-hour battery life because to the S9 SiP's efficiency.

The S9 SiP in the Apple Watch Series 9 is the company's most advanced watch processor to date, and it's paired with a new 4-core Neural Engine that's twice as fast at machine learning.

The Double-Tap Feature

The Digital Crown and Taptic Engine are only two of the innovations that make Apple Watch so easy to use, coupled with actions like tapping, swiping, raising your wrist, and covering the display to silence sound. With Apple Watch Series 9, users may operate the device with one hand and without touching the screen by use of a new double tap gesture. Many of Apple Watch Series 9's most useful features are activated by a double touch of the watch hand's index finger and thumb.

For example, you may halt a timer, play and pause music, or snooze an alarm by double-tapping the app's main button. You may use the gesture to capture a picture with Apple Watch's Camera Remote or to answer and finish phone calls. From the watch face, you can open the Smart Stack with a double tap, and another double touch will navigate through the stack's widgets.

The speedier Neural Engine in Apple Watch Series 9 analyses data from the accelerometer, gyroscope, and optical heart sensor using a new machine learning technique to allow the new double tap gesture. When the index finger and thumb double-tap, the algorithm picks up on the subtle motions of the wrist and the resulting variations in blood flow. In a software upgrade coming next month, you'll be able to use the double tap gesture.

With Apple Watch Series 9, users may operate the device with one hand and without touching the screen by use of a new double tap gesture. By repeatedly tapping an app's main button, you may do actions like answering calls, pausing and resuming playback, pausing an alarm, and more.

Display

The maximum brightness of the Apple Watch Series 9 display is up to 2000 nits, twice that of the Series 9 model, making it easier to see text in direct sunlight thanks to the power-efficient S9 SiP and sophisticated display design. The brightness may be set as low as 1 nit for use in dark environments or first thing in the morning.

The Series 9 Apple Watch can become as bright as 2000 nits, which is twice as bright as the Series 9 model.

Siri And Health App

Siri queries now be fulfilled locally on Apple Watch for the first time. Siri does not depend on Wi-Fi or cellular networks to provide faster and more accurate replies for tasks that do not need information from the internet, such as beginning a workout or setting a timer. Dictation is up to 25% more accurate than with Apple Watch Series 9 thanks to the Neural Engine's processing capabilities.

Siri may now access data from the Health app for questions about health and fitness in a private and safe manner thanks to on-device processing. Ask about your blood glucose level if you have a linked monitor, how many hours of sleep you had the night before, or how far along you are in closing your Activity rings. Apple Watch Series 9 users can now use Siri to track vitals including weight, menstruation, and medication intake.

Precise Location
Finding one's iPhone with the help of an Apple Watch is a popular function. For the iPhone 15 series, Precision Finding is now possible thanks to

the S9 SiP's incorporation of a second-generation Ultra Wideband (UWB) processor. Precision Finding helps locate a missing iPhone by providing distance and direction information as well as visual, tactile, and auditory cues, even if the phone is in a different room.

The S9 SiP chip's second-generation Ultra Wideband enables Precision Finding, which may help you locate your lost iPhone from across the room by delivering distance and direction information as well as visual, tactile, and auditory cues.

UWB also allows for greater Apple Watch and HomePod interaction. Apple Watch Series 9 will automatically activate Now Playing to control the media when the user is within four meters of a playing HomePod. If HomePod is idle, the Smart Stack will default to featuring recommended material.

Watchos 10 Features

The watchOS 10 that powers the Apple Watch Series 9 is a major upgrade.

- A new way to see data with rethought programs and the Smart Stack, which only displays the widgets that are required at the moment.
- Snoopy, Palette, and Solar Analog are three wonderful new watch faces. Nike has released a new watch face called Nike Globe, which illuminates the globe's lines as time passes.

- New cycling workouts, stats, and Workout Views are all possible now that Bluetooth connection is available for power meters, speed sensors, and cadence sensors.
- On the iPhone, a cycling session might pop up as a Live Activity and take up the whole screen when pressed.
- Improve your outdoor activities with the new Compass Waypoints and Maps features.
- The Mindfulness app's ability to register current mental state as an additional tool for supporting mental wellness.
- The ambient light sensor may be used to keep tabs on how much time an individual spends outside, which has been linked to a lower risk of myopia and other positive effects on physical and mental health in people of all ages.
- WatchOS 10 adds a new feature called Smart Stack to the Apple Watch, which displays useful widgets at the precise moment they are required.

Environment-Friendly Designs

The Apple Watch Series 9, the Apple Watch Ultra 2, and the Apple Watch SE, in certain case and band configurations, are the company's first carbon neutral products. Apple Watch's carbon impact has been drastically reduced as part of Apple 2030. The three largest contributors to greenhouse gas emissions—materials, power generation, and transportation—have all had their emissions cut. High-quality carbon credits from initiatives rooted on nature are used to counteract the remaining, negligible emissions. All new Apple Watch boxes are made from recycled materials, and a new emblem designates carbon neutral devices.

Watchbands

Apple's new FineWoven fabric is a high-end microtwill manufactured from 69 percent post-consumer recycled fiber and is more durable and hypoallergenic than leather. FineWoven may be purchased with both the Magnetic Link and the Modern Buckle bands and has a suede-like texture.

Apple has decided to stop using leather in all of its new products, including watch bands, effective immediately.

The well-liked Sport Loop band has been revamped to use 92% recycled yarn. The carbon footprint of the all new Apple Watch Sport Loops is zero.

Apple collaborated with Nike and Hermès to create eco-friendly shoe and handbag lines. Each Nike Sport Band is now constructed with at least 32% recycled fluoroelastomer, thanks to the inclusion of multicolored flakes generated from surplus bands that form a randomized pattern, while the Nike Sport Loop, which has a space-dye design, repurposes yarn from prior seasons.

Seven distinct Apple Watch Series 9 models are shown, each with a Nike Sport Loop or Nike Sport Band in a variety of colors.

A new line of Hermès bands is inspired by the brand's legacy in the textile industry. Toile H, an adaptation of the label's distinctive checkered canvas, and Twill Jump, a deep solid hue with contrasting features, are two new woven bands. Kilim is constructed of sporty, waterproof molded rubber and features a deployment buckle, while Bridon is the first knitted band for Apple Watch, with a hand-braided, chevron-patterned design. These four new bands are paired with the timeless new Hermès Radial watch face.

HOW TO PAIR YOUR IPHONE & APPLE WATCH

You will need an iPhone 9 or later running iOS 16 to utilize your Apple Watch with watchOS 9. Both the iPhone and Apple Watch include setup assistants that can help you get set up.

VoiceOver and Zoom can assist with the Apple Watch and iPhone setup, too, if you have trouble seeing the screen.

The Apple Watch must be activated, paired, and configured.

1. Don your Apple Watch and wear it proudly. If you want your Apple Watch to fit snugly yet

comfortably on your wrist, just choose the appropriate band size from the menu.

2. Press and hold the side button until the Apple logo appears to switch on your Apple Watch.
3. Close the distance between your iPhone and Apple Watch, and when the iPhone's screen displays the Apple Watch pairing screen, touch Continue.

   You may also go to the Apple Watch app on your iPhone and choose Pair New Watch from there.

4. Choose Set Up for Me in the Apple Watch App.
5. Position your iPhone so that the Apple Watch is visible in the Apple Watch app's viewfinder. This mates the two gadgets together.
6. Select Setup Apple Watch, and then complete the process by following the prompts on your iPhone and Apple Watch.

While your Apple Watch is syncing, you may learn more about it by selecting Get to Know Your Watch. This user guide, as well as the latest news and information on Apple Watch, are all accessible from your iPhone. This data may be accessed after setting up your Apple Watch by opening the Apple Watch app on your iPhone and selecting the Discover tab.

Next to one other, an iPhone and an Apple Watch. Your iPhone now displays "Apple Watch is Syncing." Syncing status is shown on the Apple Watch.

How To Turn On Mobile Service

Setup for your Apple Watch includes the option to enable cellular data. You may turn it on in the Apple Watch app on your iPhone later if you change your mind.

Both your iPhone and Apple Watch need to be activated on the same cellular network. However, if you're setting up an Apple Watch for a family member, the watch may utilize a different cellular provider than the iPhone you're using to operate it.

Not everything has access to cellular networks.

How To Pair Apple Watch

- When attempting a pairing, if you see a watch icon: You have an iPhone that is synced with your Apple Watch. You'll have to delete everything on your Apple Watch and then reset it.
- In the absence of a pairing prompt from the camera: Follow the on-screen directions by selecting Pair Apple Watch Manually from the iPhone's bottom menu.

How To Re-Pair Your Apple Watch

1. Launch the Apple Watch app on your iOS device.
2. Select My Watch, and then touch All Watches in the menu bar.
3. Select the Apple Watch you want to de-pair by tapping the Info button next to it and then selecting Unpair Apple Watch.

Combine Several Apple Watches

If you already have an Apple Watch, you may use the same method to link a second one. Close the distance between your iPhone and Apple Watch, and when the connection screen for your Apple Watch appears on your iPhone, hit Pair. Alternatively, do as follows:

1. Launch the Apple Watch app on your iOS device.

2. Select My Watch, and then touch All Watches in the menu bar.
3. Select Add Watch and then proceed with the on-screen prompts.

How To Quickly Switch To A New Apple Watch

When you're in range, your iPhone will automatically pair with any Apple Watch you're wearing. Try raising your wrist while wearing a different Apple Watch.

Apple Watches may also be selected manually:

1. Launch the Apple Watch app on your iOS device.
2. Select My Watch, and then touch All Watches in the menu bar.
3. Disable the Automatic Switch.

Apple Watch owners may check the status of their iPhone connection by touching and holding the bottom of the screen, swiping up to access Control Center, and tapping the connected symbol.

The active Apple Watch.

On the Apple Watch app's All Watches screen, a tick indicates which Apple Watch is currently being used.

Connect New iPhone To An Apple Watch

If your Apple Watch is currently connected to an older iPhone and you wish to transfer that pairing to your new iPhone, you may do so by following these instructions:

1. You may back up the iPhone that is associated with your Apple Watch by using iCloud Backup.
2. Prepare your new iPhone for use. Select the most recent backup from the drop-down menu under

"Restore from iCloud Backup" on the Apps & Data screen.
3. During the remainder of the iPhone setup process, choose the option to pair your Apple Watch with your new iPhone.

After setting up your iPhone, you'll get a notification on your Apple Watch asking you to pair it. When prompted, enter your Apple Watch passcode after tapping OK.

Move Your Existing Mobile Phone Service

If you already have a cellular Apple Watch, you may transfer your current cellular plan to a new cellular Apple Watch by following these steps:

1. You can use the Apple Watch app on your iPhone to control your watch while you're wearing it.
2. Select "My Watch," "Cellular," and then "Info" next to your cellular plan.
3. Select the carrier from the list, and then tap Remove Plan.
   To deactivate this Apple Watch from your mobile plan, you may need to get in touch with your service provider.
4. Put on your second Apple Watch, which has cellular connectivity, take off your previous watch, hit My Watch, and then tap Cellular.

Get your watch set up for cellular by following the on-screen prompts.

APPLICATION FOR APPLE WATCH

You can change watch faces, tweak the Dock, add applications, and more through the Apple watch app on your iPhone.

Apple's Watch application icon

How To Launch The Apple Watch Software

1. Select Apple Watch from your iPhone's app list.
2. Select "My Watch" to see the Apple Watch configuration screen.

You'll only see the settings for the currently selected Apple Watch if you have more than one synced with your iPhone.

Swipe to see your watch fac collection.

Settings for Apple Watch

The default screen for the Apple Watch app on the iPhone is called My Watch, and it displays your watch faces at the top and your settings towards the bottom. The Apple Watch app has three tabs at the bottom of the screen: My Watch (for customizing your Apple Watch), Face Gallery (for browsing the many watch faces and complexities), and Discover (for reading up on the ins and outs of Apple Watch).

How To Charge Apple Watch

Prepare the battery pack.

1. Put your charger or charging wire on a level table in a well-ventilated environment.

The Apple Watch Magnetic Fast Charger to USB-C Cable (for Series 7 and Series 9) or the Apple Watch Magnetic Charging Cable (for all previous versions) is included with your Apple Watch purchase. If you don't have an Apple Watch Magnetic Charging Dock, you may use a MagSafe Duo Charger instead.

2. Connect the power cord to the wall outlet using the appropriate adaptor.
3. Insert the adaptor into a wall outlet.

Rapid charging is not yet accessible everywhere.

Charge Your Apple Watch

If you have an Apple Watch Series 7 or later, you can use the Apple Watch Magnetic Fast Charger to USB-C cable, while older versions can use the Apple Watch Magnetic Charging Cable. The Apple Watch is held in place while charging thanks to a concave end on the charging cable that magnetically attaches to the rear of your device.

If your Apple Watch isn't in quiet mode, you'll hear a chime and see a charging icon appear on the display when you plug it in. Apple Watch's power indicator flashes red when it's low on juice and turns green when it's fully charged. The Apple

Watch charging icon appears yellow while in Low Power Mode.

Your Apple Watch may be charged either lying flat, with the band open, or on its side.

- The Apple Watch Magnetic Charging Dock and the MagSafe Duo Charger need the watch to be laid flat during charging.
- If your battery is critically low, your screen may display a charging cable and a picture of the Apple Watch Magnetic Fast Charger to USB-C Cable or Apple Watch Magnetic Charging Cable.

Series 9 Apple Watch

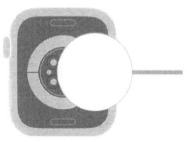

Apple's Watch Magnetic Fast Charger to USB-C Cable has a concave end that magnetically attaches to the rear of the device.

How To See Battery Power

Holding down the bottom of the screen and swiping up will bring up Control Center, where you can check your battery life. Installing a battery complication on the watch face is a simple way to see how much juice is left.

Watch dial with a % of battery life complication.

How To Enable Low Power Mode

To save power, go to Low Power Mode. Performing this action disables the Always-On Display, as well as any background blood oxygen or heart rate monitoring and alerts. Emergency alerts may not go through, and there may be problems with other notifications and with your cellular or Wi-Fi connectivity. The cellular connection is disabled unless it is needed, such as while playing music stream or sending a text message.

When the battery reaches 90% capacity, Low Power Mode will automatically be disabled.

This screen displays the remaining charge of any Bluetooth-linked battery-operated gadgets, such as AirPods, that are attached to your Apple Watch.

When your Apple Watch's battery life reaches 10 percent or less, you'll get a warning and have the option to switch to Low Power Mode.

Switch Back To Regular Power Mode
1. To access Control Center, press and hold the bottom of the screen.
2. To disable Low Power Mode, just tap the battery percentage.

Time since the last charge should be verified.

The Apple Watch's battery settings now indicate an 94% charge. Battery life as shown via a graph.

1. Launch the Apple Watch's Settings menu.
2. Battery Tapping.

   The remaining battery percentage, a graph detailing the recent history of the battery charge, and the time and date of the previous battery charge are all shown on the Battery screen.

Check Battery Health

Learn how much juice is left in your Apple Watch's battery compared to when it was brand new.

1. Launch the Apple Watch's Settings menu.
2. Select the battery and then Battery Health.

If your Apple Watch's battery life has considerably decreased, you'll get a notification to help you decide what to do next.

Don't let applications auto-reload in the background.

The previously-used app is closed and no longer uses any resources when you move to a different app, although it may "refresh" (check for updates and new material) in the background.

Background app refreshes might be energy intensive. Turning this feature off will save battery life significantly.

1. Launch the Apple Watch's Settings menu.
2. Select "Background App Refresh" under "General"
3. To stop all applications from refreshing in the background, you may turn off Background App Refresh. Alternatively, you may scroll down and disable refresh for certain programs.

The background app refresh option won't affect apps that have complications on the active watch face.

ACTIVATE AND AWAKEN YOUR WATCH

Activate and deactivate your Apple Watch.

- If your Apple Watch is turned off, you may turn it on by pressing and holding the side button until the Apple logo displays (after a brief period of a blank screen).

Turning on Apple Watch brings up the watch face.

- Press and hold the side button until the sliders display, then hit the Power button in the upper right, and finally drag the Power Off slider to the right to switch off your Apple Watch.

You may check the time even while your Apple Watch is off by pressing and holding the Digital Crown.

The toggle to turn off the power on the Apple Watch. To disable Apple Watch, move the slider to the left.

Your Apple Watch will stop charging if you turn it off. First, unplug your Apple Watch from its power source.

At all times operational

The Always On option may be found on the Display & Brightness settings menu.

If you have an Apple Watch that supports it, putting your wrist down won't prevent the watch face from showing the time. Raise your wrist to activate Apple Watch in its entirety.

Always On is disabled in Low Power Mode on your Apple Watch. Tap the screen to bring up the watch face.

Apple Watch Series 5, Series 6, Series 7, and Series 9 users may take use of Always On.

1. Launch the Apple Watch's Settings menu.
2. Choose Always On from the Display & Brightness menu.
3. The following settings may be adjusted once Always On has been activated.
- Select Complicacies That Display Information When Your Wrist Is Down.

- Select which alerts will be shown when you put down your wrist.
- Select which applications will be shown when you put down your wrist.

How To Wake The Screen On Your Watch

The Apple Watch display may be awakened in the following ways by default:

- Raise one hand. When you put your arm down, your Apple Watch goes back to sleep.
- Use the Digital Crown or tap on the screen to navigate.
- Activate the Digital Crown and raise it.

If you don't want your Apple Watch to wake up when you lift your wrist or move the Digital Crown, you can disable this behavior in the Settings app by going to Display & Brightness.

Use theater mode to temporarily disable the Apple Watch's wrist-raising wake feature.

If your Apple Watch isn't waking up when you elevate your wrist, check that the wrist and watch orientation you choose match. Your Apple Watch may require charging if tapping the display or pressing or turning the Digital Crown does not activate it.

Take A Look At The Clock Again

When using an Apple Watch app, you may customize how long it takes until the watch returns to the clock face.

1. Launch the Apple Watch's Settings menu.
2. To set a certain time for your Apple Watch to revert to the clock face, choose General > Return to Clock and then scroll down to the appropriate time. In either 2 minutes or 1 hour, always.
3. Pressing the Digital Crown takes you back to the time display.

The time you choose will be used by all applications by default, but you may change this. Select an app from the list, then touch Custom, and finally select a preference.

Awaken To Your Last Task

Apple Watch may be programmed to resume use from where it left off in several applications. Audiobooks, maps, meditation, music, now playing, podcasts, stopwatches, timers, voice memos, walkie-talkies, and workouts are just some of the applications available.

1. Launch the Apple Watch's Settings menu.

2. Select an app from the drop-down menu, then activate Return to App by going to Settings > General > Return to Clock.

Stopping whatever you were doing in the app (a podcast, a Maps route, a timer) will bring you back to the clock face.

If you'd rather use your iPhone, open the Apple Watch app, choose My Watch, then select General > Return to Clock.

How To Increase Display Time

When you touch the Apple Watch to wake it up, you may leave the screen on for a longer period.

1. Launch the Apple Watch's Settings menu.
2. Select Display & Brightness, then Wake Duration, and finally the 70-second option.

HOW TO LOCK AND UNLOCK WATCH

Open Apple Watch

Apple Watch may be unlocked either by inputting a password or automatically when your iPhone is unlocked.

- Type in the security code: Apple Watch has to be woken up and the passcode entered.

- Apple Watch is unlocked when the iPhone is unlocked. To enable Unlock with iPhone, launch the Apple Watch app on your iPhone, then go to My Watch > Passcode > Passcode.

  To activate Apple Watch Touch ID, your iPhone must be within regular Bluetooth range (approximately 33 feet or 10 meters). Apple Watch requires a password to be entered if Bluetooth is off.

You need not use the same passcode on your Apple Watch as you do on your iPhone.

How To Modify Your Watch Password

You may modify your Apple Watch passcode using the Turn Passcode Off button, the Change Passcode button, and the Unlock with iPhone switch.

Following these instructions, you may modify the Apple Watch passcode you put up initially:

1. Launch the Apple Watch's Settings menu.
2. Follow the on-screen instructions after selecting Passcode > Change Passcode.

You can also access this feature by launching the Apple Watch app on your iPhone, selecting My Watch, tapping Passcode, and finally selecting Change Passcode.

If you want to use a passcode that is more than four digits long, you may disable Simple Passcode in the Settings app on your Apple Watch.

Deactivate The Security Code
1. Launch the Apple Watch's Settings menu.
2. Select Passcode, and then select Disable Passcode.

To disable the passcode on your Apple Watch, launch the Watch app on your iPhone and go to My Watch > Passcode > Turn Passcode Off.

Apple Pay cannot be used if the password protection on your Apple Watch is turned off.

Self-Locking Mechanism
When you take off your Apple Watch, it will automatically lock itself. Follow these steps to modify how your wrist is detected.

1. Launch the Apple Watch's Settings menu.
2. To activate or deactivate Wrist Detection, tap Passcode.

When wrist recognition is off, several Apple Watch capabilities are lost:

- To enter your passcode and approve a purchase using Apple Pay on your Apple Watch, double-click the side button.
- There is a lack of data for several indicators of Activity.
- Notifications and monitoring of heart rate have been disabled.
- There will be no more automatic locking and unlocking of the Watch.
- Even if Apple Watch detects a hard impact fall, it will not immediately dial 911.

Manually Lock Control Center

You may manually lock Control Center by clicking the lock symbol in the corner.

1. To access Control Center, press and hold the bottom of the screen.
2. Select "Lock" from the menu.

Disable wrist detection if you want to manually lock your Apple Watch. To disable wrist detection, go to the Apple Watch's Settings > Passcode > Turn Passcode Off.

The next time you attempt to use your Apple Watch, you'll be prompted to enter a passcode.

You may prevent inadvertent touches while working out by locking your screen. Lock your Apple Watch by swiping right when using the Workout app. Water Lock prevents accidental unlocking of your Apple Watch when swimming.

If You Lose Your Secret Code

You need to factory reset your Apple Watch if you lose your password. Here are several methods to do that:

- If you want to reset your Apple Watch and forget the passcode, you'll need to unpair it from your iPhone and then pair it again.

- You may try reconnecting your Apple Watch to your iPhone after resetting it.

Delete Apple Watch after 10 failed tries to unlock it.
If your Apple Watch is lost or stolen, you may secure your data by setting it to delete all of its contents after 10 failed passcode tries.

1. Launch the Apple Watch's Settings menu.
2. To delete all data, choose the Passcode option.

If you have an Apple Watch and a Mac with macOS 10.12 or later, you can use it to unlock your computer.

SWITCHING LANGUAGES AND ORIENTATIONS

Apple Watch supports switching languages and orientations.

Pick A Language Or Country
You may choose the language that is shown on your Apple Watch if you have your iPhone set up to utilize several languages.

1. Launch the Apple Watch app on your iOS device.
2. Select a language by tapping My Watch, then General, Language & Region, and Custom.

Below "Preferred Languages," the Apple Watch software displays English and Spanish. This is the Language & Region screen.

Swap The Direction Of Your Wrists
Swap the direction of your wrists or Digital Crown

You may change the orientation of your Apple Watch so that it responds to a raise of the wrist to wake it and turns the Digital Crown in the desired direction if you wear it on the other wrist.

1. Launch the Apple Watch's Settings menu.
2. Select Settings, then Orientation.

The Apple Watch app on the iPhone may also be accessed in this way: touch My Watch > General > Watch Orientation.

Apple Watch's orientation screen. Both the wrist and the Digital Crown may be customized.

HOW TO REMOVE, REPLACE, & RE-FASTEN BANDS

Remove, replace, and secure your bands following these guidelines.

Use a band that is the same size as your Apple Watch case. The Apple Watch Series 4, Apple Watch Series 5, Apple Watch SE, Apple Watch Series 6, Apple Watch Series 7, Apple Watch SE (2nd Generation), and Apple Watch Series 9 are all compatible with bands made for the original Apple Watch or the first three generations of Apple Watch. You may interchange the bands on your 39mm,

40mm, and 41mm watches, and the bands on your 42mm, 44mm, and 45mm watches without any problems.

Bands made for Apple Watch Series 4, Series 5, Series 6, Series 7, Series 9, Series SE (2nd Gen), Series 8, and Series 9 may be used with every Apple Watch up to and including Series 9. The Apple Watch Series 4, Apple Watch Series 5, Apple Watch SE, Apple Watch Series 6, Apple Watch Series 7, Apple Watch SE (2nd Generation), and Apple Watch Series 9 are compatible with the Solo Loop and Braided Solo Loop bands. Bands made for the first three generations of Apple Watches may be used with the Series 4, Series 5, Series 6, Series 7, Apple Watch SE (2nd Gen), and Apple Watch Series 9.

How To Remove Bands

1. Keep your finger on the Apple Watch band button.
2. Just slip the old band out of the way and the new one in to replace it.

Never try to jam a band into the opening. Repress the band release button if you encounter any resistance when removing or installing a band.

The Apple Watch in two pictures. The button used to free yourself from the band is seen on the left. The band hole on the right has the watch band only halfway inserted.

Put On A Band

The Apple Watch functions best when it is snug on the wrist.

To use the Apple Watch's wrist recognition, haptic alerts, and heart rate sensor, the back of the device must be in direct touch with your skin. Maintaining comfort and allowing the sensors to function properly by finding the sweet spot between too tight and too loose while wearing your Apple Watch. In addition, the Apple Watch's sensors are ineffective unless it is worn on the upper part of the wrist.

CHAPTER TWO

HOW TO INSTALL A WATCH FOR A RELATIVE

For example, if your parent or kid is too young to have their own iPhone, you may set up and maintain their Apple Watch for them. You can only create a Family Sharing group if you are the group's organizer or a legal guardian.

To access the Apple Watch's settings and download software updates, the iPhone you used to connect and set it up must be within the typical Bluetooth range (approximately 33 feet or 10 meters). The individual in your Family Sharing group who you are setting up Apple Watch for must have a cellular-enabled Apple Watch SE or Apple Watch Series 4 or later. (The family member's watch need not be on the same network as the iPhone you use to control it.).

The family setup option is currently only accessible in certain locations.

You can control the following with the help of the Apple Watch app and the Screen Time feature on your iPhone:

- The Bounds of Communication and Its Security
- A plan for taking breaks from technology
- The Apple Watch has a mode called "Schooltime" that disables or hides some functions during school hours.
- Configuration of web-based email and scheduling apps like iCloud and Google Calendar
- Restrictions on inappropriate material, shopping, and personal information

Depending on the Apple Watch's configuration, you may also be able to examine its Activity, Health, and Location data.

There are restrictions on how an Apple Watch set up for a family member communicates with the iPhone used for setup. You can't pass over chores from the managed Apple Watch to the iPhone, for example, or unlock a family member's associated iPhone from the Apple Watch you set up for them. It's not possible to erase an app from an iPhone that was used to set up an Apple Watch for a family member.

Install Watch For A Relative

It's just as easy to set up an Apple Watch for a loved one as it is for yourself. Erase the watch to make sure it is completely blank before pairing and setting it up for a family member.

1. Demand that a relative don their Apple Watch. You may make the Apple Watch snug without being uncomfortable by adjusting the band or selecting a different band size.
2. Press and hold the side button until the Apple logo displays to turn on Apple Watch.
3. Get your iPhone within range of the Apple Watch, wait for the iPhone to display the Apple Watch pairing screen, and then touch Continue.

Alternatively, you may launch the Apple Watch app on your iPhone, choose My Watch, then All Watches, and finally Add Watch.

Apple's Watch application icon

4. Select Family Member Setup, and then touch Continue.
5. If you're using the Apple Watch app on your iPhone, you'll need to put it in a position where the Apple Watch can be seen in the viewfinder. This mates the two gadgets together.
6. Select Apple Watch Setup. To complete the setup, just follow the on-screen prompts on your iPhone and Apple Watch.

Control a Watch belonging to a loved one.

1. Launch the Apple Watch app on the iPhone serving as the watch's main controller.
2. Select My Watch, then Family Watches, then a specific watch, and finally, Done.

Settings for a monitored watch may be accessed through the My Watch button.

Setting	Options
General	Check for updates, change language and region, and reset Apple Watch.
Cellular	Set up cellular if you haven't.
Accessibility	Configure accessibility settings.
Emergency SOS	Turn on or off the option to hold the side button to call emergency services, and add and change emergency contacts.
Schooltime	Set up a Schooltime schedule.
Screen Time	Manage parental controls, get insights about your family member's screen time, and set limits.
Activity	Manage a fitness experience made for younger users.
Contacts	Choose trusted contacts.
Find My	Choose notification settings.
Handwashing	Manage restrictions, and turn the handwashing timer on or off.
Health	Add or edit health details and Medical ID, view the health data (with the proper permissions and settings) of the person who uses the managed Apple Watch, request to share health data, and choose to stop receiving health data.

Heart	View the heart data (with the proper permissions and settings) of the person who uses the managed Apple Watch, including heart rate, heart rate variability, resting heart rate, and walking heart rate average.
Mail & Calendar	Add a family member's account—Gmail or Outlook, for example. Also choose how often Apple Watch fetches calendar updates.
Messages	Choose dictation options, and edit smart replies.
Noise	Turn Environmental Sound Measurements on or off, and set the noise threshold.
Photos	Select a photo album from the iPhone used to manage the watch, and choose the number of photos Apple Watch can display.
Wallet & Apple Pay	Set up Apple Cash and Express Transit cards.

Not all Apple Watch capabilities that you may enable in the iOS Settings app will be accessible on a managed Apple Watch.

Schedule Your Screen Time

Set up parental controls on an Apple Watch using Screen Time. Screen Time allows you to set limits on how much time a user spends online and which people or applications they may talk to. You may set restrictions on in-app purchases, mature material, and location services via the iTunes Store.

Here's how to establish Screen Time:

1. Launch the Apple Watch app on the iPhone serving as the watch's main controller.
2. Select My Watch, then Family Watches, then a specific watch, and finally, Done.
3. To activate Screen Time, choose it from the menu, then hit the Settings cog.
4. Allowable material, communication security, screen time limitations, and app/website exclusions may all be set on the subsequent screens.
5. Make a password for Screen Time.

An iOS device's Downtime configuration screen. There's a timed switch up there. The drop-down

menu includes choices like Every Day and Customize Days; Every Day is now chosen. The screen's center displays the hours "from" and "to," while the screen's lower portion has a Block at Downtime button.

You can also access Screen Time via the Settings app on your iPhone by selecting it, then tapping the name of a family member under the Family heading, then Turn On Screen Time, and finally configuring Screen Time.

START USING WATCH & SCHOOLTIME

Schooltime's analog clock faces the date and digital time shown in the watch's middle. The user's name is listed on the watch's base.

The Apple Watch app Schooltime disables several functions throughout the school day so that parents and other caregivers can concentrate.

Schedule Classes

1. Launch the Apple Watch app on the iPhone serving as the watch's main controller.
2. Go to "My Watch," "Family Watches," and then choose a timepiece.
3. Select the end, then the time for school.
4. Then, choose Edit Schedule after switching to Schooltime.
5. Set Schooltime to go into effect on your watch at the hours and on the days that you like.
6. If you'd want to create separate schedules for different times of day, such as 9:00 a.m. to noon and 1:00 p.m. to 3:00 p.m., tap Add Time.

The Schooltime editing interface on an iPhone. You may choose from Every Day, Every Weekday, and Customize Days, and Right Now it's Set to Every Weekday. The screen's center displays a pair of hours, "From" and "To," with "Add Time" located just below.

Stop Going To Class

If a member of your family has to leave Schooltime—say, to look at their activity rings—they can.

Select "Exit" by tapping the screen, then pressing and holding the Digital Crown.

When you lower your wrist, the Schooltime watch face will appear again if you leave the app within the designated school hours. Until the next planned start time or until you hit the Schooltime button in Control Center, Schooltime will be dormant during non-scheduled hours.

Track The Release Of Schooltime

You will get a report detailing the time and duration of your family member's leave from Schooltime. Here's what you need to do to access the report:

1. Launch the Apple Watch app on the iPhone serving as the watch's main controller.

2. Go to "My Watch," "Family Watches," and then choose a timepiece.
3. After tapping "Done," choose "Schooltime" to get reports detailing when and for how long Schooltime was activated.

   The report is available on the Apple Watch as well. To access it, go to your Apple Watch's Settings > General > Date & Time > Schooltime.

When the screen goes to sleep, school time begins anew.

If your child is attending an after-school study group that meets outside of Schooltime's normal operating hours and would like not to be interrupted while studying, they may switch on Schooltime at any time. To access the Schooltime setting, press and hold the bottom of the screen, then slide up to the Control Center. Schooltime may be left by holding the Digital Crown and selecting Exit. Once the time has been set or activated in Control Center, the school will resume.

HOW TO LISTEN TO MUSIC ON APPLE WATCH

Listen to Apple Music on your managed Apple Watch via Wi-Fi or cellular if you're a member of a Family Sharing group that has a family subscription.

1. The first step is to launch the Music app on your monitored Apple Watch.
   - Select the Listen Now button to hear music handpicked just for you.
   - To listen to Apple Music Radio or a specialized channel, choose Radio.
   - Select Music from Apple Watch by tapping Library.
   - Select Search, then enter (only Apple Watch Series 7 and Apple Watch Series 9) or sketch the name of an artist, album, or playlist.
     Scribble is currently only accessible in English.
   - Choose from a collection of songs curated especially for young listeners by the experts at Apple Music.
   - Choose from any saved albums or playlists on your Apple Watch.
   - To play and choose music, use the Music app's controls or the Now Playing app's controls.

2. Listen to podcasts on an Apple Watch under management.

Subscribe To And Play Podcasts

An Apple Watch under management may be used to subscribe to and play podcasts.

Siri Podcast Playback

Just tell Siri, "Hey, play the podcast Wild Things." The newest edition of the podcast is playing on your Apple Watch.

Try To Find A Podcast

1. Launch the Podcasts application on the watched Apple Watch.
2. Select the Search tab, type in the podcast's name, and then select it.

Select Follow to subscribe to the program. You may play an episode by tapping on it.

VIEW FAMILY'S' HEALTH & ACTIVITY REPORTS

Once daily activity objectives have been established, you may check in to see how active a family member was. If your loved one permits you, you may see their medical records as well.

Create A Plan

Create a plan to get a family member moving.

Managed Apple Watches for kids to set activity targets in terms of "move minutes" rather than "active calories." Children under the age of 13 may participate in outdoor run, walk, and bike exercises designed just for them. The exercise aim centers on minutes of vigorous activity (such as running, leaping, and playing).

Regardless of the wearer's actual age, an Apple Watch administrator may switch the wearer's fitness experience from the "under 13" to the "over 13" category.

1. To control the watch, use the Apple Watch app on the iPhone.
2. Go to "My Watch," "Family Watches," and then choose a timepiece.
3. Simply choose "Done," then "Activity," and then toggle "Under 13 years old" on or off.

To do so on an Apple Watch, the family member only has to go to the Settings menu, choose Activity, and toggle "Under 13 years old" on or off.

Study A Log Of Events

1. To track your loved one's progress toward their new fitness objectives, use the Health app on your iPhone.
2. Click the Sharing button, and then choose the relative's name from the Sharing with you drop-down menu.
3. Perform an Action.
4. By tapping the timeline, you may observe the relative's daily activities up to that point in time.

Daily, weekly, monthly, and yearly views of activity data are all available.

Refer To The Health Resources

If your loved one has permitted you, you may monitor their hearing health and heart rate in addition to their activities.

1. Launch Sharing in the Health app on your iOS device.
2. To share with a family member, choose their name from the Sharing With You menu.
3. Select a Health Category by tapping its tab.

Include Medical Information & A Photo ID

Here's what to do if you forgot to include a loved one's medical information during setup:

1. Launch the Apple Watch app on the iPhone serving as the watch's main controller.
2. Go to "My Watch," "Family Watches," and then choose a timepiece.
3. Select Health from the menu that appears once you hit "Done."
   - You may add or change details about your health by selecting the Health Details tab.
   - To add emergency contacts and other information, choose Medical ID, then select Edit.

Both the iPhone used to run the Apple Watch and the watch itself displays health information and Medical ID.

- For the iPhone user: To see a loved one's profile, open Health, choose Sharing, and then touch the person's name.
- Regarding the monitored Apple Watch: Launch the Apple Watch's Settings application and choose the Health option.

INITIATE APPLE CASH FAMILY
Pay for a loved one's Apple Watch purchase with Apple Cash Family.

If you're the group administrator for Family Sharing, you may enable Apple Cash allowing your group's younger members to use their Apple Watches to make in-app purchases and give and receive funds over Messages. You may set restrictions on the people your kid can send money to, get alerts if they make a purchase, and even disable access to their account entirely.

Apple Cash is only compatible with the iPhone SE and subsequent models (iPhone 6 and later).

Apple Pay Setup For A Family

The family members you're setting up Apple Cash for must be under the age of eighteen, and you must be the organizer of the family to do so.

1. Tap "Settings" > "[your name]" > "Family Sharing" on your iPhone.
2. Select a kid or adolescent and then tap Apple Cash.
3. Follow the on-screen prompts to create an Apple Cash account by selecting Set up Apple Cash.

A member of your family in the United States may use Apple Pay to send and receive money, as well as make purchases.

Control Apple Pay With Your Watch
Family members may manage Apple Pay on their shared Apple Watch.

1. Launch the Wallet app on the iPhone serving as the watch's controller.
2. Click the More button after tapping your Apple Cash card.
3. Choose a member of the family by tapping their name.
4. Prepare the following choices:
   - You get to decide who in the family may get the money.
   - You may choose to get alerts whenever a close relative makes a purchase.
5. To use Apple Pay to transfer money, open the Messages app and tap the button labeled "Send Money."

Select Lock Apple Cash to stop the person from using Apple Pay or transferring money over Messages.

Touch Transactions here or open the Wallet app on your iPhone and touch your Apple Cash card to see the purchases made by other family members. You may see the financial dealings of your loved ones by selecting Latest Transactions or Transactions in [year].

ACCESS WATCH SOFTWARE

You may launch any Apple Watch app from the Home Screen. The Dock allows you to quickly launch frequently-used programs. Up to ten of your most frequently used programs may be permanently installed in the Dock.

Exhibit Your Applications
Exhibit your applications as a list or a grid.

The Home Screen supports both a grid and a list layout for its app presentation. Here's how to choose the right one:

1. Press and hold the Home button.
2. Pick between a grid and a list layout.

The View Options window with the Grid View and List View buttons is clearly shown. The Apps Edit button may be found at the bottom of the display.

Launch Programs From The Main Menu
How an app launches is determined by the current view.

- To switch to grid view, choose the app's icon. To launch the app that is now in the middle of the screen when viewing the Home Screen, just rotate the Digital Crown.

From the watch face, press to see the Home Screen.

Tap to open an app.

A Watch's home screen displays as a grid, grouping applications. Launch a program with a tap. Easily access a wider selection of applications by dragging the screen.

- Presented in a list format: Tap an app icon and rotate the Digital Crown.

List view of Apple Watch's home screen, displaying installed applications. Launch a program with a tap. If you want to view more options, keep scrolling.

Press the Digital Crown once to exit an app, and then press it again to access the watch face (or touch the watch symbol in grid view to access the Home Screen).

While in another app or the watch face, double-clicking the Digital Crown will launch the previous app used.

Use The Dock To Launch An Application

1. A spin of the Digital Crown will take you to the next app in the Dock once you press the side button.
2. Launch an app with a tap.

The calendar app on the Dock with the All Apps button below. If you rotate the Digital Crown, you may access more software options. One may be accessed by tapping on it.

Set The Dock's Contents To Your Liking
The Dock may display either your most recently used applications or up to ten of your most often used apps.

- Access recently used software: Launch the Dock app on your Apple Watch and choose Recents to access the recently used settings. The Dock displays the currently active application at the top, followed by the most recently used applications in reverse chronological order.
Apple Watch Recents may also be accessed from the iPhone app by selecting My Watch from the Dock menu.

- Examine the programs you enjoy: Launch Apple Watch on your iPhone, choose My Watch, and finally select Dock. To add applications to your Favorites list, go to the Favorites menu, click Edit, and then press the Plus button. To rearrange them, click the Reorder button and drag it. When you're done, press the Done button.
- Press the side button, then use the Digital Crown to choose the app you wish to delete from the Dock. Tap the app's X button and swipe left.

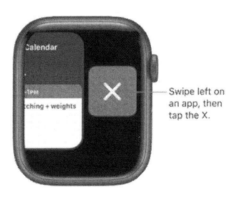

Swipe left on an app, then tap the X.

Swiping left on an app will reveal the Dock, with the X button located on the right.

- Replace the Dock with the Home Screen: Move your cursor to the very end of the Dock and then click All Apps.

Whether you've opted to display Recents or Favorites, applications that have active sessions (such as a Maps navigation session or a Workout session) will always be shown at the top of the list.

ARRANGE WATCH APPLICATIONS

Arrange Your Apps In A Grid Layout

1. To access the Apple Watch's Home Screen, just push the Digital Crown.

   To switch from list view to grid view, touch and hold the Home Screen. Alternatively, you may use Grid View from the App View menu in Settings on your Apple Watch.

2. Tap and hold an app, and then choose Edit Apps.
3. To reposition the app, just drag it.
4. When you're ready to stop, just press the Digital Crown.

Touch and hold an app, then drag to a new location.

Apple Watch's home screen is presented as a grid.

The Apple Watch software may also be accessed from the iPhone by selecting My Watch > software View > Arrangement. Drag and drop an app icon to a new spot after touching and holding it.

In the list view, applications are always sorted alphabetically.

Touch and hold, then drag to move apps around.

The Apple Watch app's Arrangement screen displays a grid of icons.

Delete An App From Your Watch

To delete an app from your Apple Watch, touch and hold the Home Screen, choose Edit Apps, and then select the X. unless you also remove it from the linked iPhone, it will stay on that device.

To uninstall an app from your Apple Watch, slide it to the left in the app list and then hit the Trash icon.

Apps on the Apple Watch may be removed in the same way they are on the iPhone. Apps, including

Apple's own, may be reinstalled through the App Store on an iPhone or Apple Watch.

Not all applications on your Apple Watch may be deleted.

Modify Your App's Settings

1. Launch the Apple Watch app on your iOS device.
2. To see the applications you've added to your watch, choose My Watch and scroll down.
3. Adjust the app's preferences by tapping it.

The Apple Watch follows the limitations you set on your iPhone under Screen Time > Content & Privacy limitations. If you turn off the Camera on your iPhone, the Apple Watch will no longer display the Camera Remote symbol.

Verify The Space That Programs Are Using

Your Apple Watch makes it easy to see how much space has been consumed, what's left, and which apps are the worst space hogs.

1. Launch the Apple Watch's Settings menu.
2. Select Preferences, then Storage.

You may also access this setting from the iPhone app by selecting My Watch > General > Storage.

Watch Time Telling

The Apple Watch has many methods of displaying time.

- Raise your wrist to see the time, which is also shown on the watch face, in the clock's grid view, and the top right corner of the majority of applications.
- Notice the hour: To activate Speak Time on your Apple Watch, go to the Settings menu, then tap Clock. To hear the time, place two fingers on the display.

On the hour, Apple Watch can also play a chime. Chimes may be activated in the Apple Watch's Settings by selecting Clock. To choose either Bells or Birds as your sound, press the Sounds button.

- You may have the time tapped out on your wrist even while your Apple Watch is in quiet mode by opening the Settings app, tapping Clock, tapping Taptic Time, turning on Taptic Time, and then selecting an option.

A Watch may be programmed to always announce the time if Taptic Time is turned off. Taptic Time requires that Control With Silent Mode be enabled in Settings > Clock > Speak Time before it can be used.

- Raise your wrist and ask Siri, "What time is it?" to check the time.

PUT YOUR WATCH INTO FOCUS MODE

Focus allows you to maintain your attention on the task at hand. Focus notifies other people and applications that you're busy and only allows you to get the alerts you wish to receive (those that match your focus).

Personal, Sleep, and Work are the three available Focus modes. Alternately, you may set up a personalized Focus on your iPhone, permitting certain contacts, limiting notifications to specific applications, and enabling or disabling time-sensitive alerts.

If you use the same Apple ID on several devices, you may have the iPhone's Focus settings synced across all of them by opening Settings, tapping Focus, and then activating Share Across Devices.

Focus On/Off Toggle

Lists of Do Not Disturb, Personal, Work, and Sleep may be found under the Focus menu. The Work Concentration is on.

1. To access Control Center, press and hold the bottom of the screen.
2. Select a Focus by touching and holding the active Focus button.

   The Do Not Disturb button appears in Control Center if Focus is not active.

3. You may focus on this task indefinitely, for an hour, till tonight/tomorrow morning, or until I depart.

Tap the Focus button in Control Center to disable it.

Focus icons show up in many places while they are active, including the top of the watch face, the app dock, and the Control Center.

Focus on what you want, and then make it happen.
1. Navigate to Settings > Focus on your iPhone.
2. Follow the on-screen prompts after tapping the Add button and selecting Focus.

   You may give your custom focus its color, icon, and name when you set it up.

Pick A Watch Dial From Focus

For each Focus, you have the option of selecting a unique watch face to be shown on your wrist. When Work Focus is on, for instance, the Apple Watch may switch to the Simple watch face.

1. Navigate to Settings > Focus on your iPhone.
2. Choose the Apple Watch icon, and then touch Set Up next to an existing Focus or Add New Focus, then Customize Focus.
3. Done once you've chosen a watch face.

Make A Plan To Concentrate

You have complete control over the timing of your Focuses on Apple Watch, and can even set them to begin at certain times of the day. The Work Focus may, for instance, begin each weekday at 9:00 am and finish at noon. Midday to one o'clock may find you without Focus or under the control of a Personal Focus. The Work Focus will thereafter resume on weekdays from 1:00 PM to 5:00 PM.

1. Launch the Apple Watch's Settings menu.
2. Select "Focus," then "Work," and finally "Add new."
3. Select the from and To boxes and specify the times that the Focus should start and stop.
4. Select the Focus's active days by scrolling down.
5. Focus may be saved by tapping in the upper left corner.
6. To add other things to the Focus, just keep doing this.

The daily schedule is shown from 9 am to 5 pm on the Work Focus screen. There's a New entry button down here.

Focus Schedule Deletion & Disablement

The following actions may be used to deactivate or remove a Focus schedule:

- Open the Settings app on your Apple Watch, go to Focus, and then press Focus to disable it. Just choose a timetable, scroll down, and disable the option to run it.

  Select enabled once you're ready to use the schedule again.

- To remove a Focus from your Apple Watch's schedule, go to the Settings app, choose Focus, and then select a Focus. Select a timetable, scroll to the bottom, and then select Delete.

MODIFY YOUR WATCH'S DISPLAY

Modify your Watch's display, font, volume, and haptics.

There is a Brightness slider at the top of Apple Watch's Display & Brightness settings, and a Text Size button at the bottom.

To modify the Apple Watch's display and brightness, launch the Settings app and go to Display & Brightness.

- Brightness may be adjusted by tapping the Brightness settings or by tapping the slider and turning the Digital Crown.
- To change the font size, choose Text Size and then press the letters or rotate the Digital Crown.
- In bold: Activate Bold Text.

Your iPhone also allows for these modifications. Adjust the brightness and font size in the Apple Watch app by opening it on your iPhone, selecting My Watch, tapping Display & Brightness, and finally making your changes.

Modify Volume

1. Launch the Apple Watch's Settings menu.
2. The Power of Touch and Sound.
3. Use the Digital Crown to fine-tune the volume by tapping the slider or buttons beneath Alert Volume.

Apple Watch's Sounds & Haptics menu, shows the Alert Volume slider and Silent Mode toggle at the top and bottom, respectively.

To adjust the volume of the alerts on your Apple Watch, open the Apple Watch app on your iPhone and go to Sounds & Haptics.

If you use headphones with your Apple Watch, you can lower the volume. Turn on Reduce Loud Sounds by navigating to Sounds & Haptics > Headphone Safety in the Settings app.

The Haptic Alerts Switch

The Haptic Alerts switch, and the Default and Prominent choices below it, allow you to customize the haptic feedback you get on your Apple Watch.

Apple Watch alerts and notifications employ haptics or wrist taps, and their intensity may be adjusted.

1. Launch the Apple Watch's Settings menu.
2. To enable haptic alerts, go to Settings > Sounds & Haptics.
3. Make a Featured or Default selection.

Alternatively, you may access the Apple Watch settings from the iPhone app by going to Watch > My Watch > Sounds & Haptics > Default or Prominent.

Toggle Digital Crown Haptics On & Off

When using Apple Watch's Digital Crown to scroll, you'll hear and feel clicks. Here's how to disable or enable these haptics:

1. Launch the Apple Watch's Settings menu.
2. Select Sound & Haptics and toggle Crown Haptics on and off.

   The haptics feedback from the system may be toggled as well.

To toggle Crown Haptics on or off, launch the Apple Watch app on your iPhone and go to My Watch > Sounds & Haptics.

The Crown Haptics display, with the toggle enabled. Turn on the haptics below to access the system.

How To Set Up Taptic Time

In quiet mode, Apple Watch will tap out the time on your wrist in a succession of individual taps.

1. Launch the Apple Watch's Settings menu.
2. Select Taptic Time by selecting Clock and then scrolling down.
3. Taptic Time may be activated and one of three modes (Digits, Terse, or Morse Code) selected.
   - Apple Watch long taps every 10 hours, then short taps every hour afterward, long taps every 10 minutes, then small taps each minute thereafter.
   - Sparse: every five hours, your Apple Watch will make a lengthy tap, then every hour and a quarter will make a small tap.
   - The Apple Watch displays the time in Morse code by tapping out each numeral.

Taptic Time on the iPhone may also be customized. To activate Taptic Time, launch the Apple Watch app on your iPhone, choose My Watch, then Clock > Taptic Time.

A Watch may be programmed to always announce the time if Taptic Time is turned off. Taptic Time requires that Control With Silent Mode be enabled in Settings > Clock > Speak Time before it can be used.

ACCESS & ACT UPON ALERTS ON YOUR WATCH

Meeting invites, texts, noise alarms, and Activity reminders are just a few examples of the types of information that might be sent to you by your apps. If you don't read a notification on your Apple Watch as soon as it arrives, it will be kept until you have some time to view it.

Act In Response To Incoming Alerts

1. Raise your wrist if you hear or feel a notification, and look at the display.

   The notification's appearance shifts from active to idle mode.

   - A banner appears at the top of the screen and the display is active.
   - When the screen is unattended, a full-screen alert will show up.
2. To check out the alert, just tap on it.

3. Swipe down on a notice to dismiss it. You may also swipe up from the bottom of the alert to dismiss it.

Apple Watch alerts the wearer to Noise. The notifications-related app's symbol displays in the upper left corner of the screen. To access the app, just touch the icon.

View Unread Alerts
View unread alerts that need action from you.

Notifications that are ignored are stored in the Notification Center until you can deal with them. If you have unread notifications, your watch face will become red. Here's what you have to do to see it:

1. You may access Notification Center by swiping down from the watch face. Touch and hold the

top of the screen then scroll down to access the other displays.

The Watch's Notification Center cannot be accessed from the Home Screen. Instead, access Notification Center by pressing the Digital Crown once you've navigated to a watch face or app.

2. To see more alerts, swipe up or down, or flip the Digital Crown.
3. You may access the notice by tapping the icon.

Siri can read your alerts aloud from Notification Center using the Apple Watch's built-in speaker or Bluetooth-connected headphones. To check your messages, just say, "Read my notifications."

Without reading it, you may dismiss a notice from the notice Center by swiping it to the left and tapping the X that appears. To dismiss all alerts at once, swipe up and choose Clear All from the menu that appears.

When using group notifications, open the group by tapping on its name, then on notice to read it.

The red dot may be disabled in the Settings app by selecting Notifications and then disabling the Notifications Indicator.

Swipe down to view unread notifications.

When you have an unread alert, a red dot will show in the exact middle of your watch face.

Mute Alerts

Apple Watch Touch users may mute their device by holding down the bottom of the screen, swiping up to reveal the Control Center, and tapping the quiet mode button.

A tap still indicates a new alert has arrived. Keep noise and taps at bay by doing the following:

1. To access Control Center, press and hold the bottom of the screen.
2. To stop all interruptions, use the Focus button.
3. Select the desired time frame by tapping Do Not Disturb and selecting either On, On for 1 hour, Tonight/Tomorrow Night, or On till I depart.

The Apple Watch may be muted in an instant simply placing the palm of your hand over the screen for three seconds whenever you get a notification. You'll get a touch on the shoulder when the mute is engaged. Cover to Mute may be activated in the Apple Watch's Settings by navigating to Sounds & Haptics and then to Cover to Mute.

CHAPTER THREE

MODIFY YOUR WATCH ALERT SETTINGS

The Apple Watch's app notifications will automatically sync with your iPhone if you haven't already done so. However, the notification settings for certain applications are flexible.

A family member's Apple Watch that you're responsible for won't follow your mirrored preferences.

Configure How Applications Notify You

1. Launch the Apple Watch app on your iOS device.
2. Navigate to Notifications by selecting My Watch.
3. Select the desired app (say, Messages) and then hit the Custom tab. Choices might involve:
   - To get push notifications from the app, please enable them in the app's settings.
   - When you send a notice to the notice Center, your Apple Watch will not vibrate or show the notification on its screen.
   - Turning off notifications disables all alerts from the app.

4. Group app alerts whichever you choose by customizing this setting. Among the available choices are:
   - Turned off: Individual notifications aren't consolidated into threads.
   - Automatically: The Apple Watch organizes its users into several categories using data from their apps. News alerts, for instance, are sorted into channels like CNN, Washington Post, and People that you choose to follow.
   - Notifications from each app are sorted into distinct folders.

The kind of alerts you get may often be customized in certain applications. You may choose which Calendar alerts you want to receive, such as when an invitation is sent or a shared calendar is updated. In Mail, you may choose which email addresses may be used for sending alerts.

The iPhone app's Notifications panel displays alerts from your Apple Watch.

Modify Alert Settings

If you swipe left on notice and then hit the More icon, you may modify additional notification settings straight from your Apple Watch. Choices might involve:

- For the next hour or the remainder of the day, your Apple Watch will not make any noise or show any alerts. Instead, they will be routed straight to Notification Center. Swipe left on a notice to see the More menu, then hit Unmute to restore the notification's visibility and sound.

- To the Summary, add: The Notification Summary is where the app's future alerts will show up on your iPhone.

  You may restore instant notifications from the app by going to the iPhone's Settings menu, tapping Notifications, selecting the app in question, and finally selecting Immediate Delivery.

- Do not use a Focus that delays most alerts if you want to get time-sensitive notifications as soon as they are sent. However, if you do not want to receive any alerts from this app at all, including those that are time-sensitive, you may disable this feature by selecting it.
- Disabling push notifications has no effect. When you launch the Apple Watch app on your iPhone, you may toggle app notifications back on by going to My Watch > Notifications > the relevant app > Allow Notifications.

The Watch alert preferences. In the upper right corner, it says "Mute for 1 Hour." Below are toggles for turning off time sensitivity, turning off, and adding to the summary.

Activate Alerts When The Screen Is Locked

The Apple Watch's lock screen may be customized to display alerts in a variety of ways.

1. Launch the Apple Watch's Settings menu.
2. Click the notification icon.
3. Pick one of the following:
   - When this option is on, your locked Apple Watch will display a summary of your notifications. The notification is summarized with the app's name and icon and a short headline.
   - When you lift your wrist to see a notification, you'll first receive a summary, followed by the complete information after a short delay.

When a new message comes, for instance, you'll first see the sender's name, followed by the message itself. If you want to prevent the whole notice from showing up until you touch it, this is the setting to use.

- By default, your Apple Watch won't alert you to new alerts if your wrist is down. If you enable this feature, alerts will display even if you're not looking at your Apple Watch.

SET UP YOUR WATCH APPLE ID

Your Apple ID profile is editable and viewable. Change your password, add a trusted phone number, add and amend your contact information, and more are all options.

Personal Details May Be Updated

1. Launch the Apple Watch's Settings menu.
2. Select [username].
3. You may perform any of the following after selecting "Name," "Phone," and "Email."
   - Rename yourself: Choose your identifying information by tapping First, Middle, or Last.
   - Look at, change, and add a contact: Look for the section labeled "Reachable At" and enter a phone number or email address there. Select the email address you want to delete, and then touch the Remove Email Address button.

- Don't forget to provide contact information: Select the desired method of contact by tapping Add Email or Phone Number, following the prompts to input an email address or phone number, and finally tapping Done.
- Put a cover over your inbox: Tap the Future.

  With this setting, you may choose to have applications contact you without sharing your actual email address. If you choose this option, Apple will generate a random email address on your behalf; any messages received to this address from the app will be sent to the address of your choice.

- Substitute Your Birth Year Select your Birthday and provide a new date.
- Access the Apple News newsletter, personalized recommendations, and more: Activating Announcements, suggestions for applications, music, TV, and more, and the Apple News Newsletter can all be found under the Subscriptions section.

Handle Apple ID Safety And Passwords
1. Launch the Apple Watch's Settings menu.
2. Select [username].

3. Then, perform one of the following after selecting Password & Security:

- Make a new passcode for your Apple ID: Select Password Change and then proceed with the on-screen prompts.

- Modify the settings for an app or website's use of "Sign in with Apple" Select an app by clicking on Apps Using Your Apple ID. To disconnect your Apple ID from the app, choose Stop Using Apple ID from the menu. (The next time you attempt to sign in using the app, you may be prompted to establish a new account.)

- To make changes to an existing trusted phone number or add a new one, press the number you want to edit or add, confirm it when required, and then hit Remove Phone Number. If you have just one trusted number, you will be prompted to input a new one before deleting the old one. Select Add a Trusted Phone Number to save an extra reliable contact number.

- If you want to sign in from a different device or iCloud.com, you'll need a verification code. Select the Verification Code button.

Check out and handle your memberships

1. Launch the Apple Watch's Settings menu.
2. Select [username].
3. Select Subscriptions, and then select an individual subscription to see its details (such as price and duration).
4. Select "Cancel Subscription" to stop your automatic payments.

You will need to cancel certain subscriptions on your iPhone.

Control And Monitor Your Hardware

1. Launch the Apple Watch's Settings menu.
2. Select [username].
3. To learn more about a certain gadget, scroll down and touch it.
4. If you don't identify the device, choose Remove from Account.

SAVE TIME USING WATCH'S SHORTCUTS

The Watch's Shortcuts app displays the "When Do I Need to Leave" and "Set Good Night" shortcuts.

You can do actions with a single touch using the Shortcuts app on your Apple Watch. You can speed up the process of doing things like finding your way home or making a top 25 playlist by creating shortcuts on your iPhone. The Shortcuts app also allows you to add shortcuts to your watch face as complications.

Apple Watch does not support all iPhone shortcuts.

Do A Quick Fix
1. Launch the Apple Watch's Shortcuts app.
2. Use the quick link.

Create A Difficult With A Short Cut

1. Simply edit the watch's face by touching and holding it.
2. Tap a problem after swiping left to the Complications page.
3. Select a shortcut by scrolling down to the Shortcuts section.

Upgrade Apple Watch with more quick-access features

1. Get out your iPhone's Shortcuts app.
2. A shortcut's More button may be seen in its upper-right corner.
3. On the shortcut screen, choose Show on Apple Watch by tapping the Info button.

PREPARE YOUR WATCH FOR HANDWASHING

The Apple Watch can detect when you begin washing your hands and encourage you to continue for the full 20 seconds, the minimum period suggested by most international health agencies. If you haven't cleaned your hands after coming home from work, your Apple Watch may remind you to do so.

Activate Handwashing

1. To activate Handwashing, go to the Apple Watch's Settings menu.
2. Select the Handwashing option and activate the Handwashing Timer.

A 20-second timer will begin counting down on your Apple Watch as soon as it recognizes that you have begun washing your hands. If you start washing your hands and stop after less than 20 seconds, you're urged to keep going.

The clock for hand washing starts at 4.

Find Out When It's Time To Wash Your Hands

Upon arriving home, Apple Watch might prompt you to wash your hands.

1. Launch the Apple Watch's Settings menu.

2. Select Handwashing, and then activate Reminders to Wash Your Hands.

Reminders to wash your hands may also be set up on an Apple Watch for a family member. To activate Handwashing Timer and Handwashing Reminders, go to the Settings app on the controlled Apple Watch, hit General, and then tap Handwashing.

Setting a home address in My Card inside the Contacts app on an iPhone is required to get handwashing reminders.

Launch the Health app on your iPhone, and choose to Browse > Other Data > Handwashing to get a report of your typical handwashing sessions.

JOIN WATCH TO A WIRELESS INTERNET CONNECTION

Many of the Apple Watch's capabilities may be used independently of your iPhone if you connect it to a Wi-Fi network.

Pick A Wireless Network

1. To access Control Center, press and hold the bottom of the screen.
2. Press and hold the Wi-Fi button, then choose a network by tapping its name.

The Apple Watch only works with 902.11b/g/n 2.4GHz Wi-Fi networks.

3. If you need to enter a password to access the network:
   - Apple Watch now has a keypad for entering passwords (only compatible with Apple Watch Series 7 and Apple Watch Series 9).
   - Scrawl the password characters with your finger on the display. You may choose capitalization and case sensitivity using the Digital Crown.
   - Select a password by tapping the Password button.
   - To input the password, please use the iPhone's keyboard.
4. Select the Join button.

Communicate Over A Secure Network

Each Wi-Fi network your Apple Watch connects to will have its private network address, or media access control (MAC) address, to help keep your data secure. You may discontinue using a private address for a network if it is unable to utilize one (for example, to give parental controls or to identify your Apple Watch as permitted to join).

1. To access Control Center, press and hold the bottom of the screen.

2. You can see which network you've joined by touching and holding the Wi-Fi button.
3. Disable your personal address book.

Keeping a Private Address enabled across all supported networks is crucial for maintaining your anonymity online. Having a secret address for your Apple Watch makes it harder to trace it when you move between various wireless hotspots.

Put Aside The Idea Of A Network

1. To access Control Center, press and hold the bottom of the screen.
2. You can see which network you've joined by touching and holding the Wi-Fi button.
3. Away with that channel!

If the network needs a password and you reconnect at a later time, you will need to input that password again.

PAIR YOUR WATCH WITH WIRELESS AUDIO DEVICES

Listen to music or podcasts on your Apple Watch using wireless headphones or speakers without needing your iPhone.

If you've already synced your AirPods with your iPhone, you can just hit play to begin listening to your favorite tunes on your Apple Watch.

Join Wireless Audio Bluetooth Devices

The Apple Watch's speaker is used for listening to Siri, phone calls, voicemail, and voice notes, therefore Bluetooth headphones or speakers are required for listening to most audio on the Apple Watch. To activate the headphones' or speakers' discovery mode, use the manual provided. Here's what to do when your Bluetooth gadget is ready to go:

1. To enable Bluetooth on your Apple Watch, go to the Settings menu.
2. If a gadget pops up, tap it.

Audiobooks, Music, Now Playing, and Podcasts all include an AirPlay button you may use to access Bluetooth settings from the play screen.

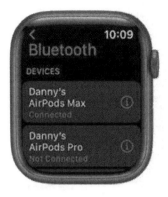

Parallel display of two monitors. The screen on the left displays a pair of linked AirPods Max and a pair of unpaired AirPods Pro that may be used over Bluetooth. The Settings menu appears on the right, with a range of options including Wi-Fi, Bluetooth, the display, and the app drawer.

Pick A Playback Method

1. To access Control Center, press and hold the bottom of the screen.
2. Click the Audio Output icon, and then choose the output device.

Listen Carefully To Your Headphones

1. To access Control Center, press and hold the bottom of the screen.
2. Tap the Headphone Volume button to adjust the volume for the headphones.

The volume of the headphones is shown on a meter.

Tone down the volume

Apple Watch allows you to set a maximum volume for your headphones.

1. Launch the Apple Watch's Settings menu.
2. To lower the volume, choose Sounds & Haptics > Headphone Safety.
3. Adjust the volume by activating the feature to lower it.

Listen To Alerts Using Your Headphones

Apple Watch will give you a headphone notice and automatically reduce the volume if you listen to your headphones at unsafely high volumes for an extended period.

Open the Health app on your iPhone, choose Browse, then touch Hearing, then select Headphone Notifications, and finally select a notification to examine its information.

Delegate From Your Watch

Handoff allows you to go from one device to another without interrupting your current task. Even while the Mail app on your Apple Watch allows you to respond to emails, you may find it more convenient to use the touchscreen keyboard on your iPhone instead. You may use Handoff with an Apple Watch that you've set up for yourself, but not with a family member's Apple Watch. To make advantage of Handoff, do as follows.

1. Get your iPhone unlocked.
2. Swipe up from the bottom edge and pause to get the App Switcher on an iPhone equipped with Face ID. (Double-clicking the Home button on an iPhone will bring up the App Switcher.)
3. If you want to access the same content on your iPhone, tap the button that appears at the bottom of the screen.

If you don't see a button in App Switcher, check your iPhone's Settings > General > AirPlay & Handoff to make sure Handoff is enabled.

By default, handoff is enabled. To turn it off, launch the Apple Watch app on your iPhone, choose My Watch, then hit General, and finally toggle off Enable Handoff.

In addition to the aforementioned apps, those that are compatible with Handoff include Activity, Alarm, Calendar, Home, Mail, Maps, Messages, Music, News, Phone, Podcasts, Reminders, Settings, Siri, Stocks, Stopwatch, Timers, Wallet, Weather, and World Clock. Your Apple Watch and iPhone must be in constant communication for Handoff to function.

You may also transfer information from your Apple Watch to a Mac running OS X 10.10 or later.

HOW TO UNLOCK A MAC WITH APPLE WATCH

Mid-2013 and later Macs running macOS 10.13 or later may be unlocked with an Apple Watch as soon as they resume activity. Both your Mac and Apple Watch must be signed into iCloud with the same Apple ID.

The model year of your Mac may be found by selecting Apple > About This Mac from the Apple menu in the upper left of your screen. Your Mac's model name will include the year it was manufactured, such as "MacBook Pro (15-inch, 2019").

Toggle On The Auto-Unlock Feature

1. Verify the following settings on your gadgets:
   - Wi-Fi and Bluetooth are both enabled on your Mac.
   - The same Apple ID is used to sign in to iCloud on both your Mac and Apple Watch, and two-

factor authentication is enabled for that Apple ID.

- There is a passcode on your Apple Watch.

2. Follow any of these options:
   - Select Apple menu > System Settings > Login Password if you're running macOS 13 or later.
   - Choose Apple menu > System Preferences on macOS versions earlier than 12. Select Security & Privacy, and then select General.
3. Tap the option to "Use Apple Watch to unlock apps and your Mac."

   Choose which Apple Watches you'd want to use to access your Mac and other applications if you have more than one.

If two-factor authentication isn't already activated for your Apple ID, follow the on-screen steps to do so, and then try again.

Mac Unlocking

You may wake up your Mac without entering a password while you're wearing your watch.

An Apple Watch display reads, "Joe's MacBook Pro Unlocked by this Apple Watch."

Have your Mac close by and your Apple Watch on your wrist with the screen open.

Use Watch As A Passcode For Your iPhone

Follow these steps to enable Apple Watch to unlock your iPhone while using Siri or when Face ID cannot be used due to an obstruction:

1. Access your iPhone's passcode by going to Settings > Face ID & Passcode.
2. Select Unlock With Apple Watch and activate your watch's security settings.
   If you wear many watches, you should activate each one separately.

3. Make sure your Apple Watch is on your wrist, turn on your iPhone, and then gaze at the screen to unlock it.

When your iPhone is unlocked, Apple Watch touches your wrist to let you know.

The display on John's Apple Watch reads: "John's iPhone Unlocked by this Apple Watch." Tap here to access the iPhone lock screen.

To use your Apple Watch to unlock your iPhone, your Apple Watch must be unlocked, on your wrist, and within range of your iPhone.

USE A CELLULAR NETWORK WITH YOUR WATCH

Without your iPhone or a Wi-Fi connection, you can still make and receive calls, send and receive messages, utilize Walkie-Talkie, listen to music and podcasts, get alerts, and more with Apple Watch with cellular and a cellular connection to the same carrier used by your iPhone.

Cellular service is not offered by all carriers in all places.

Integrate Watch With Your Phone Service

By following the on-screen prompts, you may enable cellular connectivity for your Apple Watch right now. Here's what you should do if you want to turn on the service later:

1. Launch the Apple Watch app on your iOS device.
2. Go to My Watch > Cellular.

If your Apple Watch has cellular connectivity, read the included instructions to activate it and learn about your carrier's service plan.

Toggle Mobile On/Off

If your iPhone is close, your Apple Watch will utilize that device's cellular connection; otherwise, it will use the Wi-Fi network to which your iPhone is already connected. Turning off cellular data may help save battery life. Just do what I say:

1. To access Control Center, press and hold the bottom of the screen.
2. You may toggle Cellular on and off by tapping its dedicated button.

When an Apple Watch has a cellular connection and you aren't carrying your iPhone, the Cellular button will light up in the color green.

Using cellular for longer periods can drain your battery faster (for more details, check out the Apple Watch's General Battery Information page). Some applications also need to be connected to your iPhone for updates.

Verify The Quality Of Your Mobile Signal

If you have access to a cellular network, you may try one of the following:

- To see how strong your cellular connection is, select the Explorer watch face, which displays information as green dots. A strong link is represented by four dots. One dot is really bad.
- Turn on the Command Room. Bars of green at the top indicate the strength of the cellular connection.
- The watch face is missing the Cellular complication.

Verify Your Data Consumption On The Go

1. Launch the Apple Watch's Settings menu.
2. Select Cellular, and then scroll down to see your data used for the current billing cycle.

Configure And Examine Your Medical Ids

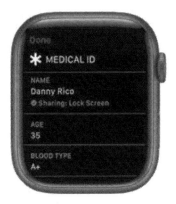

The Apple Watch's Medical ID screen displays the wearer's name, birth date, and blood type. When the user checks the box next to their name on the lock screen, others may access their Medical ID. The task may be completed by clicking the Done button in the upper left corner.

You may carry vital information about yourself, such as allergies and medical issues, on a Medical ID in case of an emergency. Medical ID information entered in the Health app on an iPhone is synced with the Apple Watch. When you utilize Emergency SOS (available in the United States and Canada) or dial 911 (available in the United States and Canada), your Apple Watch may transmit your Medical ID to the appropriate authorities.

Your Medical ID may be displayed on your Apple Watch, making it easily accessible to first responders.

Here are the steps you need to take to access your Medical ID on your Apple Watch:

1. To bring up the sliders, press and hold the side button for a few seconds.
2. Raise the Medical ID bar to the top.
3. When you're done, press the Done button.

Alternatively, you may access SOS > Medical ID from the Settings app on your Apple Watch.

CHAPTER FOUR

HOW TO USE YOUR WATCH TO GET IN TOUCH WITH 911

Get aids fast using your Apple Watch to make emergency calls.

Follow any of these options:

- Sliders may be accessed by holding the side button down until they appear; once they do, the Emergency Call slider can be moved to the right.

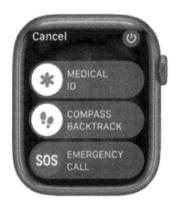

On the Apple Watch display, the Medical ID, Compass Backtrack, and Emergency Call sliders may be adjusted. On the far right, you'll find the power button.

In an emergency, your Apple Watch will contact the appropriate authorities, such as 911 in the United States. (In certain countries/areas, you may need to dial a number on the keypad before you can make a call.)

- Keep holding the side button until you hear an alarm and see a countdown appear on your Apple Watch. Your Apple Watch will automatically contact 911 when the countdown timer reaches zero. If you're in a dangerous situation and don't want to alert others, use the Emergency Call slider to initiate a call to emergency services without the watch counting down.

  Turn off Automatic Dialing if you don't want your Apple Watch to dial 911 for you when you push and hold the side button. To disable Hold Side Button, go to the Settings menu on your Apple Watch and navigate to SOS > Hold Side Button. You may also disable Hold Side Button to Dial by opening the Apple Watch app on your iPhone, selecting My Watch, tapping Emergency SOS, and finally tapping Cancel. The Emergency Call slider is still available for use in case of an urgent call.

- Simply tell Siri, "Hey, I want to call 911."

- To dial 911 from your Apple Watch, launch Messages, choose New Message, press Add Contact, then the number pad button. Create a new message by selecting the appropriate option and sending it.

If you have Fall Detection turned on, and Apple Watch detects a heavy fall and you remain motionless for roughly a minute, it will try to contact emergency services.

After 20 seconds, if your Apple Watch detects a catastrophic automobile collision, it will inform you and make an emergency call.

If you have an Apple Watch Series 5 (GPS + Cellular), Series 6 (GPS + Cellular), Series 7 (GPS + Cellular), or Series 9 with cellular service, you can use it to make an emergency call from many different areas. If your Apple Watch is not activated, is not compatible with or configured to operate on a specific cellular network, or is not set up for cellular service, that network may not accept an emergency call from your Apple Watch Series 5, Apple Watch SE, Apple Watch Series 6, Apple Watch Series 7 (GPS + Cellular), or Apple Watch Series 9.

Add in case of emergency contacts. If you do not terminate the emergency call before it concludes, your Apple Watch will send a text message to your emergency contacts. For a certain amount of time, after you activate SOS on your Apple Watch, your emergency contacts will be alerted whenever your location changes.

Your watch will connect to the appropriate local emergency services when you initiate an Emergency SOS call when traveling internationally, but it will not share your position or send a text message to your emergency contacts. It is possible to make international emergency calls without having activated cellular service on the watch in some countries and locations.

Put An End To An Urgent Call
If you accidentally placed an emergency call, you may terminate it by tapping the End Call button twice.

Make sure your alternate contact information is up to date.

First responders will visit your emergency location if they are unable to find you.

1. Launch the iPhone's Settings menu.

2. To change your emergency contact information, go to Settings > Wi-Fi Calling > Update Emergency Address.

CONTROL WATCH'S FALL DETECTION FEATURES

If you have Apple Watch set up with Fall Detection and it detects a heavy fall, it will call emergency services and notify the people you've designated as emergency contacts. Apple Watch will tap your wrist, sound an alert, and try to notify emergency services if it detects a heavy fall and that you have remained immobilized for roughly a minute.

To make an emergency call, your Apple Watch or nearby iPhone must be connected to cellular data or have Wi-Fi calling enabled and Wi-Fi coverage.

Where Emergency SOS via satellite is available, Fall Detection will utilize your iPhone to transmit the notice when cellular and Wi-Fi connectivity is unavailable and your iPhone 14 or iPhone 14 Pro or later is close to your Apple Watch.

The safety check for falls is displayed.

When you set up your Apple Watch (or connect it to the Health app on your iPhone), Fall Detection is activated automatically if your birthday shows that you are 55 or older. You may manually activate Fall Detection if you're between the ages of 19 and 55:

1. Launch the Apple Watch's Settings menu.
2. Select "SOS" and then "Fall Detection" to activate the feature.

   The Apple Watch app on the iPhone may be accessed by going to My Watch > Emergency SOS > Fall Detection.

   Even if Apple Watch detects a heavy impact fall, it won't automatically try to summon emergency services if you've turned off wrist detection.

3. Select "Always on" if you want Fall Detection to be active at all times, or "Only on during workouts" to activate it just after you've begun exercising.

Fall Detection during workouts is enabled by default on a new Apple Watch running watchOS 9.1 or later if the user is between the ages of 19 and 55. Updating an older Apple Watch to the latest watchOS requires turning on the functionality to detect heavy falls only during workouts.

However, not all falls can be detected by the Apple Watch. High-impact exercise that might mimic a fall is more likely to set off Fall Detection as you increase your level of physical activity.

Control Watch's Collision Detection System
In the event of a catastrophic vehicle accident, your Apple Watch Series 9 or Apple Watch SE (2nd Generation) may assist link you with emergency services and alert others you've designated to receive notifications.

If your Apple Watch detects a catastrophic vehicle accident, it will inform you and, after 20 seconds, dial 911 unless you cancel. If you are unconscious, it will play an audio message for the police and fire departments explaining that you were in a serious automobile accident and providing your precise location along with a rough estimate of the search area.

To make an emergency call, your Apple Watch or nearby iPhone must be connected to cellular data or have Wi-Fi calling enabled and Wi-Fi coverage.

Crash Detection alerts to emergency services may be conveyed using the Emergency SOS via satellite system, where Emergency SOS via satellite is available, if your iPhone 14 or iPhone 14 Pro or later is close to your Apple Watch and cellular and Wi-Fi coverage are unavailable.

Crash Detection won't cancel out any preexisting emergency calls if a major automobile accident is detected.

Adjust The Setting For Crash Detection

By default, Crash Detection is enabled. After a serious vehicle accident, you may disable Apple's warnings and automated emergency calls by following these steps:

1. Launch the Apple Watch's Settings menu.
2. To disable Call After Severe Crash, go to SOS > Crash Detection.

TRACK YOUR BLOOD OXYGEN LEVELS

Use your Apple Watch to track your blood oxygen levels

The Blood Oxygen monitor is ticking down from 9 seconds while it takes a reading.

If you have an Apple Watch Series 6 or later, you may use the Blood Oxygen app to determine how much oxygen your blood cells are transporting from your lungs. How effectively your blood is oxygenated is a good indicator of your general health.

The Blood Oxygen app isn't accessible everywhere. The results of the Blood Oxygen app are not meant for diagnostic purposes.

1. Launch the Apple Watch's Settings menu.

2. Blood Oxygen should be selected, and then Blood Oxygen Measurements activated.

When in Sleep Focus or Theater mode, stop taking readings in the background.

A bright red light flashes on your wrist to assess blood oxygen levels, which may be easier to see in the dark. If the light from the measures is bothersome, you may disable them.

1. Launch the Apple Watch's Settings menu.
2. You may disable In Sleep Focus and Theater Mode by selecting Blood Oxygen from the menu.

Check Your Oxygen Saturation Levels

If background measurements are enabled, the Blood Oxygen app will collect readings at set intervals throughout the day; otherwise, you may take a reading whenever you choose.

1. Launch the Apple Watch's Blood Oxygen app.
2. Put your hand flat on a table or your lap and your arm straight out, with the Apple watch screen facing up.
3. After pressing the Start button, keep your arm perfectly motionless for the whole 15 seconds.
4. When the test is complete, you get the results. Select the End button.

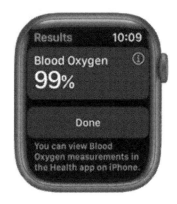

An oxygen saturation level of 99 percent is shown on the Blood Oxygen test screen. Please click the completed button below.

You must touch your skin with the rear of your Apple Watch. Successful Blood Oxygen readings are more likely when the Apple Watch is worn in a comfortable, but not too loose, fashion that allows the skin to breathe.

Examine past readings of your blood oxygen level

1. Launch the iPhone's Health application.
2. Select Respiratorily, then Blood Oxygen from the Browse menu.

PUT YOUR WATCH'S CALCULATOR TO USE

The Calculator software allows you to conduct simple mathematical operations. Tip amounts and check splits may also be readily determined.

What is 73 multiplied by 9? - Siri. Also "What is 19% of 225?"

The Calculator app on an Apple Watch. The display is a standard numeric keypad with the usual math keys located to the right. There is a row of buttons at the top that reads "C," "+," and "-."

Make A Fast Calculation

1. Launch the Apple Watch's Calculator app.
2. Make a combination of taps and key-ins to see the outcome.

Divide the bill, and decide on a gratuity.

1. Launch the Apple Watch's Calculator app.
2. Put in the total price of the bill and then click the tip button.
3. Select a tip amount with the turn of the Digital Crown.
4. Select the number of persons who will be splitting the cost by tapping persons, and then turning the Digital Crown.

Each person's share of the bill, including the tip, as well as the overall amount, are all shown.

The Tip function is not accessible everywhere.

If you delete the Calculator app from your iPhone, it will also be deleted from your Apple Watch.

SCHEDULE CHECKS AND EDITS

The Apple Watch's Calendar app displays your upcoming and historical events (in List and Day view) for the next six weeks and two years. The Apple Watch may display events from any or all of the calendars synced with the iPhone.

A screenshot of a calendar with the event's information.

Siri: Ask a question like, "What's my next event?"

Check Out Your Schedule

1. To see upcoming events, choose the date from the watch face or use the Calendar app on your Apple Watch.
2. Use the Digital Crown to flip through a calendar of forthcoming activities.

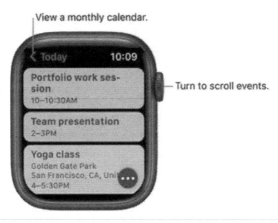

Display the day's schedule on a calendar.

3. If you tap an event, you'll be able to view its time, place, attendees, and any associated notes.

   A quick touch in the upper left corner will take you to the following function.

Your schedule may be seen monthly or weekly.

How To Modify The Calendar App Display
You may toggle between views in the Calendar app by opening it, tapping the More icon, and then selecting a different view.

- Next: Displays the week ahead of time for your convenience.
- The happenings for the current day are shown.
- Timeline: Displays everything happening in your life from the last two weeks to the future two years.

In the Day view, swipe left or right cycles through the days; in the List view and Up Next view, turn the Digital Crown cycles through the options.

Simply tapping the time at the top right of the screen will take you back to the present day and time.

The calendar interface, with the Up Next button at the top and the Day, Week, and List views below.

Calendars Of Weeks And Months

You may switch between the week and month views while perusing the calendar in Day or List view. Launch the Apple Watch's Calendar app and execute one of the following:

- Indicate the current week: Select the upper left of the screen.
- Change the week displayed: Tap the left or right side of the screen.
- Present a week's worth of activities: Click a weekday on the calendar.
- Present the actual month: Tap the in the upper left corner when the current week is shown.
- Alter the month displayed: Rotate the Screen Crown Digital.

- Pick any week of the month: Make a week of it.

Simply Insert A New Happening

The Calendar app on your iPhone will automatically sync with your Apple Watch whenever you add an event. The watch itself may be used to schedule things.

- Siri can help you out. Create a May 20th, 4 pm, FaceTime with Mom calendar event by saying something like "Create a calendar event."
- When using the Apple Watch Calendar app, choose an event in the Up Next, Day, or List view, press the More button, and then hit New Event. Enter the event's title, description, start and finish times, and attendees, as well as which calendar you'd want to add it to, and then press Add.

A new appointment is on the calendar. The event's name appears at the top, followed by a Location

*text box. There's an "All-day" option in the footer.
There's a button labeled "Start Date" down here.*

Swap out a date or time

- To get rid of a planned gathering: Select an event,
  press Delete, and then repeat.
  You have the option of canceling just this one
  occurrence or all of them if this is a series.
- To modify an event, use the iPhone's Calendar
  app.

React to a request made using Calendar

You may react to event invites on your Apple Watch
either immediately upon receipt or at a later time.

- If the invitation reaches you: To accept, decline,
  or maybe the notice, scroll to its very bottom.
- What to do if you find the alert much later: Select
  it from the alerts feed, scroll down, and tap to
  reply.
- For those who have already opened the Calendar:
  To react to the event, tap on it.

press the organizer's name in the event information,
then press the appropriate phone, message, email,
or Walkie-Talkie button to get in touch with the
event's organizer.

Discover How To Go To A Function

Your Apple Watch may lead you to an event's location if one is specified.

1. Launch the Apple Watch's Calendar application.
2. Select an activity and then the location.

Modify The "Leave Now" Messages

If an event specifies a location, your Apple Watch will send you a "leave now" notification depending on how long it will take you to get there given the current traffic. Select a time window, say, two hours before the event, by doing the following:

1. Launch the iPhone's Calendar application.
2. Listen to the show.
3. Select a new time frame by tapping Alert.

Modify Your Schedule Accordingly

Follow these steps to modify the calendar alerts you get and choose which calendars will be shown on your Apple Watch:

1. Launch the Apple Watch app on your iOS device.
2. Select Calendar by selecting My Watch first.
3. Choose Notifications > Calendars > Custom.

HOW TO TRACK MEDICATIONS USE ON A WATCH

The Health app on your iPhone is where you can keep track of all the pills, powders, and capsules you consume. You may register your prescriptions and set reminders in the prescriptions app on your Apple Watch.

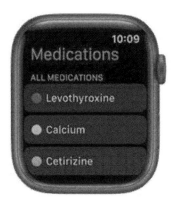

A complete medicine list is shown by the Medications app.

The Medications function is not meant to replace your doctor's advice. Medication labels may provide supplemental information, but you should always check with your doctor before making any changes to your treatment plan.

Schedule Your Medications On Your iPhone

1. To see your medications, launch the Health app on your iPhone, hit Browse in the bottom right, and then choose Medications.
2. Select Add Medication or Add a Medication to create or add to your list, respectively.
3. One of the following should be done to determine the medication:

   - You may enter the name here: Add by tapping the search box, typing the name, and tapping Search.

     You may get recommendations as you type in the United States. You may choose a suggested name or type the name in full and then hit Add.

   - Take a picture: (in the USA only, on the iPhone SE 2nd gen and later, the iPhone XS, and the iPhone XR) Follow the on-screen prompts by tapping the Camera icon to the right of the search bar.

     If no results are returned, choose Search by Name and enter the name in the search bar.

4. Identify prospective encounters, create a visual identifier, and establish a timetable by following the on-screen prompts.

Track Your Prescriptions

Medication records are shown in the Medications app.

Medications may be scheduled in the Health app on the iPhone, and your Apple Watch will send you notifications when it's time to take them. This is how you keep track of your medicine intake.

1. A medicine log notice may be accessed by tapping the notification. Or else, use the Apple Watch's Medications app.
2. Look at the present pattern of medicine use, such as the pills you take first thing in the morning.
3. Choose to Record Taking Everything.

   Apple Watch keeps track of when you took medicine, how many units you took, and what you took it for.

4. Scroll down, choose a drug from Your Medications, and then touch Log to record only that dose.

   Under Logged, you'll see the medication's name and when it was last taken.

5. Touch the drug you want to edit, and then touch Taken or Skip, and finally hit Done.

On your iPhone, launch the Health app, choose Browse, and then select Medications to see the log and your medication history.

HOW TO SELECT A PHOTO ALBUM & HANDLE THE STORAGE

Select a picture album and handle space allocation on your Watch.

You can browse images from any album on your iPhone, as well as see highlighted photos and Memories, using the images app on your Apple Watch.

Pick The Album To Save On The Watch

The Watch app on the iPhone allows you to choose the album to save on the Apple Watch Photos settings, with the Photo Syncing option located in the center and the Photos Limit setting located below that.

The default picture album for the Apple Watch is the one you've labeled "Favorites," but you may modify this if you choose.

1. Launch the Apple Watch app on your iOS device.
2. Select the album from the Photos tab, then sync it by tapping My Watch.

Open the Photos app on your iPhone, then delete the image from the album you've synchronized with your Apple Watch.

Use the iPhone's Photos app to create a fresh album only for Apple Watch snaps.

Display Highlights Reels And Recollections

Photos and Memories that are highlighted on your iPhone will be synced to your Apple Watch automatically.

1. Launch the Apple Watch app on your iOS device.
2. Select "My Watch," "Photos," "Sync Memories" or "Sync Featured Photos" to activate the features.

We must put an end to photo synchronization

Follow these steps to prevent your iPhone from syncing photographs from the Memories, featured, or selected albums:

1. Launch the Apple Watch app on your iOS device.
2. You may disable photo syncing by selecting My Watch > Photos > Off.

Reduce Watch's Capacity For Pictures

Your Apple Watch can only hold as many photographs as its storage allows. You may reduce the number of pictures saved on it so that more room can be made available for music or other media.

1. Launch the Apple Watch app on your iOS device.
2. Select My Watch, then Photos, then Photos Limited.

One of the following will reveal the number of pictures stored on your Apple Watch:

- To see your Apple Watch's serial number, open the Settings app and go to General > About.
- Go to General > About in the Apple Watch app on your iPhone by tapping My Watch.

Open the Settings app on your Apple Watch and go to General > Storage to see the percentage of storage used up by your photographs. Launch Apple Watch on your iPhone, then touch My Watch, followed by General > Storage.

Capture A Watch Image

1. To enable screenshots on your Apple Watch open the Settings app and go to General > Screenshots.
2. To capture an image of the display, hold down the Digital Crown and the side button at the same time.

Your iPhone's screenshots will be stored in the Photos app.

CHAPTER FIVE

HOW TO USE PICTURES

You may use Apple Watch's Photos app to go through your photo library and choose a photo to use as your watch face.

Photos' home screen for Apple Watch showcasing a grid of images.

Check Out Photos On Your Watch

Check out snaps on your Watch via the Photos app.

Launch the Photos app on your Apple Watch and scroll through your photo library using these gestures.

1. Select a photo from a previously synced album or Featured Photos on your Apple Watch.
2. If you want to see a picture, tap on it.
3. To navigate through the gallery, swipe left or right.
   - You may zoom in and out of photos by turning the Digital Crown and swiping.
   - If you want to view the whole picture album, you need to zoom out.

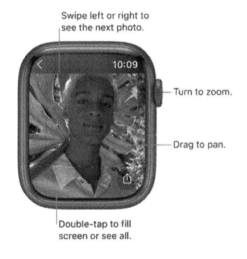

Swipe left or right to see the next photo.

10:09

Turn to zoom.

Drag to pan.

Double-tap to fill screen or see all.

You may use the Digital Crown to zoom in on an image, the touchpad to pan around, and a double tap to see the whole image or expand it to fill the screen. To view the following picture, swipe left or right. In the right-hand corner, there's a 'Share' button.

Review An Old Photo Right On Your Wrist

The Apple Watch's Siri and Photos watch faces now support viewing Memories, in addition to the Photos app.

- The Siri watch face displays a recent recollection: Select the Siri watch face and bring up a certain moment.
- The Photos watch face displays images from the Memories album. Launch the Apple Watch app on your iPhone, choose Face Gallery, then select Photos to watch Face, and finally select Dynamic.

The dynamic watch face automatically refreshes with new photographs from your most recent Memories.

Check Out A Live Photo On Your Watch

To activate a picture's live features, touch and hold the photo after finding the Live picture icon in its lower left corner.

Put Up A Picture

To choose a sharing method when viewing a picture in the Photos app on your Apple Watch, hit the Action button.

Make A Custom Picture Watch Dial

Photos on the Apple Watch may be edited by tapping the Action button, scrolling down, and selecting Create Face. In the Apple Watch app on your iPhone, you may make a Kaleidoscope watch face based on the picture or add a new Photos watch face.

Customizing your iPhone's watch face is a breeze. You may make a Portraits, Photos, or Kaleidoscope watch face by opening the Photos app on your iPhone, tapping a picture, tapping the Action button, swiping up, and tapping Create Watch Face.

PUT YOUR WATCH TO USE AS A MEDITATION TOOL

Using the Apple Watch's Mindfulness app, you may take a few minutes each day to concentrate on your breathing and establish a deeper connection with yourself and the world around you. Listen to guided meditations on your Apple Watch with an Apple Fitness+ membership.

Get Some Quiet Time To Think
Get some quiet time to think or breathe.

Launch the Apple Watch's Mindfulness app and choose one of the following:

- To reflect, choose Reflect, read the topic, and zero in on it before selecting Begin.
- To take a breath, just press the Breathe button, inhale as the animation expands, and exhale as it contracts.

You may cancel a session at any time by swiping right and selecting the End option.

Meditation prompts like "Find something close to you" are shown in the Mindfulness app. Take note of the specifics. The option to get started is down below.

Determine How Long A Session Will Last

1. Get out your Apple Watch and fire up the Mindfulness app.
2. Select a time frame by selecting the More option, then Duration.

There's a range of options from one to five minutes.

The opening screen of the Mindfulness app, with a timer reading one minute at the top. A Reflect session may be improved by following the advice below.

Modify Your Mindfulness Preferences

You may adjust the pace at which you breathe in and out, as well as the haptics and the frequency with which you are reminded to practice mindfulness.

Select Mindfulness in the Apple Watch's Settings menu and then perform one of the following:

- Remind yourself to be present: Change the settings for Start of Day and End of Day under Reminders, and then add new reminders by tapping Add Reminder.

- Turn on/off Weekly Summary to start or stop receiving a weekly summary.
- To silence today's mindfulness prompts, choose "Mute for today."
- Modify the rate at which you breathe: Select the desired breath rate by tapping the corresponding Breath Rate button.
- Tap Haptics, and then choose between None, Minimal, or Prominent for the haptics effect.
- Access updated meditations: When your Apple Watch is charged, you may download new meditations by activating Add New Meditations to Watch. Once you've finished a meditation, it will be removed automatically.
- You can also access this feature by opening the Apple Watch app on your iPhone, selecting My Watch, then tapping Mindfulness.

Keep an eye on your pulse while practicing mindfulness.
Do some quiet thinking or breathing. The Summary page displays your current heart rate.

Your heart rate data may be seen at a later time. To check your heart rate, open the Health app on your iPhone, choose Browse, then Heart. Select Show Additional Heart Rate Data, slide upwards, then select Breathe.

Put On Your Watch's Breathe Dial

You may access mindfulness practices on your wrist with the Breathe watch face.

1. To keep the current watch face on the screen, touch and hold the screen.
2. Tap the New button (+) once you've swiped to the left.
3. Rotate the Digital Crown to bring up Breathe, and then press Add.
4. The Mindfulness app may be accessed by tapping the watch's face.

Breathe is the watch's face.

LISTEN TO GUIDED MEDITATIONS

You can now use your Apple Watch to listen to guided meditations (with an Apple Fitness+ membership).

With an Apple Fitness+ subscription and your Apple Watch, AirPods, or any set of Bluetooth headphones or speakers, you may listen to guided meditations.

Apple Fitness+ is currently only available in certain markets.

Launch A Meditative Audio Program

1. Get out your Apple Watch and fire up the Mindfulness app.
2. Use the Audio Meditations from Fitness+.
3. You may scroll up and down to look at different parts of the meditation.

   Near the end of each episode, you'll find information on the episode's subject, instructor, and meditation length.

4. If you want to read more about the meditation, save it to your collection, or listen to its playlist in the Music app, tap the Information icon.
5. To start a meditation, just tap on one.

Apple Watch displays the elapsed duration of the meditation and your current heart rate as it plays.

While a guided meditation is playing, you may stop it by swiping right and selecting stop or End. Tap

Workout, and then choose a workout to begin while the meditation plays in the background.

Look through all of your finished meditations.
When you've finished a whole meditation, it will be stored in My Library in the Fitness app on your iPhone and Apple Watch.

1. Get out your Apple Watch and fire up the Mindfulness app.
2. Use the Audio Meditations from Fitness+.
3. To see previously listened-to meditations, swipe down and choose My Library.
4. You may see the meditation's details, download it, delete it, or listen to its playlist in the Music app by tapping the Info icon.
5. You may replay any meditation by tapping on it.

The Apple TV, iPhone, or iPad may also be used to peruse the contents of My Library. Go to your device's My Library and open the Fitness app (Fitness+ on the iPhone).

HOW USE YOUR WATCH TO MONITOR YOUR PULSE

Checking your heart rate is a good indicator of your overall health. At any moment, you may see your resting, walking, exercising, and post-workout heart rates, as well as your heart rate during a Breathe session.

Keep your wrist and Apple Watch free of dirt and moisture. A poor recording might be the result of perspiration and water.

Keep An Eye On Your Pulse

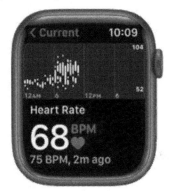

The Heart Rate app's main interface, displays the user's current heart rate in the bottom left corner, their previous reading in smaller text below it, and a chart illustrating their heart rate at various times of the day, in the upper right corner.

To check your current, resting, and walking average heart rate, launch the Heart Rate app on your Apple Watch.

As long as you're wearing your Apple Watch, it will keep tracking your heart rate.

Find a representation of your pulse rate data

1. The Apple Watch has a useful Heart Rate app; launch it.
2. You may see your average heart rate when walking, at rest, or by tapping the appropriate button.

Open the Health app on your iPhone, choose Browse, then hit Heart, and finally select an item to see your heart rate statistics over a longer period. Heart rate information from the past hour, day, week, month, or year may be shown.

Start Recording Your Heart Rate

When using the Heart Rate app, working exercise, or engaging in a session of Breathe and Reflect, your Apple Watch will automatically be monitoring your heart rate. If you have previously disabled heart rate monitoring, you may enable it again.

1. Launch the Apple Watch's Settings menu.
2. Navigate to Health > Privacy & Security.
3. Select the Heart Rate option and toggle it on.

You can also see your Heart Rate by opening the Apple Watch app on your iPhone, selecting My Watch, and then Privacy.

Apple Watch Series 6, Series 7, and Series 9 only: The back of your Apple Watch must be in touch with your skin for wrist identification, haptic alerts, and blood oxygen level readings. Maintaining comfort and allowing the sensors to function properly by finding the sweet spot between too tight and too loose while wearing your Apple Watch.

MAINTAINING A HEALTHY HEART

If anything out of the norm happens to your heart, your Apple Watch can alert you. If, for instance, you haven't moved in 10 minutes but your heart rate is over or below a certain threshold, your Apple Watch might send you a notification.

When you initially use the Heart Rate app or at any other time, you may choose to enable notification of your heart rate.

If your Apple Watch detects a potentially dangerous abnormal heart rhythm, such as atrial fibrillation (AFib), you may be alerted to the issue. Your Apple Watch may provide insight into how often your heart has AFib if you have previously been diagnosed with this arrhythmia. Your illness may be affected by things in your lifestyle, which you may monitor.

Get Alerts When Of Your Heart Rate
Get alerts when your heart rate is too high or too low.

A warning that your heart rate is too high.

1. Launch the Apple Watch's Settings menu and choose the Heart option.
2. Set a heart rate threshold by selecting High Heart Rate Notifications or Low Rate Notifications.

The Apple Watch app on the iPhone may also be accessed by selecting My Watch and then Heart. Select Extremely High or Extremely Low Heart Rate, and then adjust the threshold.

Get Alerts About Arrhythmias
Get alerts about arrhythmias (may not be accessible in your location).

If Apple Watch detects a potentially dangerous abnormal heart rhythm, such as atrial fibrillation (AFib), it may send you a notice.

1. Launch the Apple Watch's Settings menu.
2. Select Heart, and then activate Notifications for Irregular Heartbeat.

To enable Irregular Rhythm, open the Apple Watch app on your iPhone, choose My Watch, and then hit Heart.

The AFib record (not accessible in all locations) will be shown.

Apple Watch displays an arrhythmia alert.

1. Select Browse in the Health app on your iPhone if you have been diagnosed with AFib.
2. Select Heart, then select Get More From Your Health, and then select Set Up under AFib History.

3. Launch the Health app, and then choose Browse, Heart, and finally, AFib History to see your AFib record.

On Mondays, your watch may send you a notice estimating how much of the previous week you spent in AFib if you wore it for at least 5 out of 7 days (12 hours each day).

Get Alerted When Of Your Cardiac Fitness Get alerted when your cardiac fitness levels are low.

During a run, stroll, or trek in the great outdoors, your Apple Watch can evaluate your cardio fitness and alert you when your heart rate drops below a certain threshold. Your cardiac fitness level might be poor, below average, above average, or high depending on your age and sex. Your Apple Watch will alert you if your cardiac fitness drops to the "Low" level. You will be notified every four months if it continues to be low.

1. Launch the Apple Watch's Settings menu.
2. To enable the Cardio Fitness Notifications, go to the Heart menu.

You can also access this feature by opening the Apple Watch app on your iPhone, selecting My

Watch, tapping Heart, and finally activating Cardio Fitness Notifications.

To check where your cardiac fitness measures place you within a range, go to the cardiac Fitness area of the Health app. To see the available Cardio Fitness Levels, click the Show All button.

VIEW NOTIFICATIONS ON YOUR WATCH

You can read incoming text messages on your Apple Watch and respond through dictation, Scribble, or a pre-written answer; you can even transfer the conversation to your iPhone to write a response if you prefer.

Check Your Watch For A Message

1. Raise your Apple Watch whenever you sense a tap or hear an alert sound to check for new messages.
2. To see the last portion of the message, just rotate the Digital Crown to the right.
3. Tap the top of the screen to read the message from the beginning.

   To read material formatted for Apple Watch, touch any website link inside a message. To see more detail, double-tap the screen.

If the message came in the past, you may access it by touching and holding the top of the screen, swiping down on the display to reveal the message notice, and then tapping it. Scroll down and click Dismiss to delete the message after reading it. Pressing the Digital Crown will silence the alert without recording the message as read.

An exchange of messages. At the very bottom, next to the text box, you'll see the App button.

View the timestamps of sent messages

To delete a message, tap the discussion in the Messages list, then swipe left on the message.

Conversations May Be Muted Or Deleted

- When in the discussion list for Messages, swipe left on the chat to mute it, and then hit the Notifications Off button.

- Remove a past discussion: To delete a chat, swipe it to the left in the Messages thread list and then choose the Trash button.

Include Media Like Photographs

You may include media like photographs, songs, and videos in your text.

Pictures, sounds, and videos may all be sent in a single message. Here's how to get at them from your Apple Watch:

- Images may be seen by tapping them, double-tapped to fill the screen, and navigated by dragging. When you're done, hit the checkmark in the upper-left corner.

  Select the individuals you wish to send the picture to or select Messages or Mail from the menu that appears when you hit the Share button. You may skip the sharing choices and just save the picture to your iPhone's Photos app by tapping Save picture. The picture may be added to a Kaleidoscope or Photos watch face by selecting Create Watch Face.

- To hear the audio, please use the play button.

  If you wish to preserve the video after it has played for two minutes, choose preserve underneath the clip before it is removed. You may extend the audio's storage on your iPhone beyond the default 30 days. To permanently delete an audio message, open its settings, choose "Messages," then "Expire," and finally "Never."

- The Music app on Apple Watch may be used to listen to any Apple Music tracks that have been sent to you in a Message. (Must have a paid Apple Music account.)
- If a message contains a video, tapping it will open it in full-screen view. Simply tapping once will bring up the media controls. To zoom out, simply double-tap and the Digital Crown may be used to change the volume. To get back to the discussion, just use the Back button or swipe left.

You may save the video by opening the message in the Messages app on your iPhone.

Pick A Notification Method

1. Get out your iPhone and launch the Apple Watch app.
2. Select My Watch, and then Messages.
3. If you want more control over how you are alerted of new messages, use the "Custom" option.

If you are using a Focus that doesn't support Messages notifications, you won't get a notice.

Set how you want to be notified.

The Watch's message preferences may be found in the iPhone app. You have the option to display alerts, activate sound and haptic feedback, and choose alert repetition.

CHAPTER SIX

HOW TO TEXT WITH APPLE WATCH

Text, photos, emoji, Memoji stickers, and audio recordings may all be included in a message created and sent using the Messages app on your Apple Watch. You may also let others know where you are by putting your location in a message, and you can pay money using Apple Pay.

Make A Watch Message

1. Launch the Apple Watch's Messages app.
2. Go up to the menu bar and choose New Message.
3. Select "Add Contact," then touch an existing contact from the list of recent chats that display, or select "Other."
   - Use the Microphone button to look for a contact or enter a phone number by voice.
   - Click the +Add Contact button to bring up your whole address book.
   - A phone number may be entered by tapping the Keypad button.
4. Choose New Message from the menu.

5. If your Apple Watch is bilingual, you may switch between languages by selecting Language and then selecting a language.

Write a message on your phone

There are several methods to write a message, and most of them just take up one screen. After entering text into the Create Message section, you may do any of the following steps:

- To use the QuickPath and QWERTY keyboard layouts: (Only compatible with Apple Watch Series 7 and Series 9; certain languages only) You may either tap the letters you want to input or use the QuickPath keyboard to glide from one letter to the next. You may terminate a word by lifting your finger.

  As you write, you'll see suggested words pop up. You may also highlight a word by tapping it, whether it's whole or incomplete, and then turning the Digital Crown for suggestions. Put your finger off the Digital Crown's turn button and go with the suggested action instead.

  To access the keyboard, slide up from the bottom of the screen and then choose Keyboard from the menu that appears.

- Send a message with only the touch of your finger using Scribble. To make changes to your message, you may use the Digital Crown to place the cursor. On the Series 7 and Series 9 Apple Watches, you can access Scribble by swiping up from the bottom of the display and then selecting the app.

Using the Digital Crown, you may touch a completed or incomplete word to highlight it, and then spin it to display suggested words. Put your finger off the Digital Crown's turn button and go with the suggested action instead.

If you have more than one language installed on your Apple Watch, you can switch to that language while using Scribble. To switch languages, swipe up from the bottom of the screen.

Not all languages have access to scribble yet.

- To dictate text, choose the Dictate option, speak your piece, and then select the Done option. It's possible to use punctuation in speech as well, as in "did it arrive question mark."

To go back to Scribble mode, either hit the Scribble button or spin the Digital Crown.

- Emoji may be added by selecting the Emoji button, selecting a commonly used emoji or selecting a category, and then scrolling through the list of available pictures. If you discover the appropriate icon, tapping it will insert it into your text.
- You may use your iPhone to type text while creating a message by receiving a prompt to use the iOS keyboard when your associated iPhone is close. To respond, tap the alert and use the iPhone keypad.

Write Messages Without Typing
Whether it's a Memoji, sticker, GIF, or audio clip, your response will stand out.

It's also possible to write messages without typing a single letter. After you've written a message, you may send it using one of these methods:

- Reply with some wit: Useful phrases are shown as you scroll; choose one with a touch and send it out.

  Open the Apple Watch app on your iPhone, choose My Watch, go to Messages > Default Replies, and then touch create Reply to create a custom response. Select "Edit," then "Drag to reorder" or "Tap to delete" to make changes to the order or remove the predetermined answers.

To switch the language of the smart responses to one you like, swipe down and choose Languages. The languages that may be typed into your iPhone are those that you have enabled in Settings > General > Keyboard > Keyboards.

- To send a picture from the Memoji Stickers collection, follow these steps: press the App icon, tap the Memoji button, select an image, hit a variant, and finally tap Send.
- Tap the App icon, then the Memoji button, scroll down, and tap More Stickers to send a sticker. Select the desired option and then hit the Send button. Messages on the iPhone are where you'll find all of your stickers and where you can make new ones.
- To send a GIF, open the App drawer, choose the GIF button, select an image, and then hit the Send button. Tap the Search area, input a search word, tap a GIF from the results, and then hit Send to send it.
- Please share a sound bite: The steps are as follows: press the App icon, tap the Audio button, record your message, hit Done, and then tap Send.

Transfer Funds With The Help Of Apple Pay

1. Select the App symbol that appears next to the iMessage field during a discussion.
2. Select the Apple Cash option.
3. Tap the Digital Crown's Send button after deciding how much money to send.
4. To send, just double-click the adjacent button.

Apple Cash isn't offered everywhere.

Use Watch To Send A Drawing

If your pals have an Apple Watch or an iPhone running iOS 10 or later, you may use Digital Touch to email them your drawings.

If someone has sent you a drawing, you may open it by tapping the alert.

1. Just type your message and choose the App button!
2. If you want to start sketching, just hit the Digital Touch button.
3. Draw directly on the screen with your finger.
4. You may choose a new hue by tapping the corresponding circle in the upper right corner.
5. If you're done with your drawing, press the Done button before sending it.

A blank white canvas with a rough sketch in the middle and a color palette selector at the top.

Use Technology To Express Your Emotions
Feel free to use technology to express your emotions.

Digital Touch allows you to communicate with others who also have an Apple Watch or iPhone running iOS 10 by sending those taps, a kiss, or even your heartbeat.

Tap the notice to see (or feel) the tap or heartbeat that was transmitted to you.

1. Start by typing your message and selecting the App button.
2. To access the sketching canvas, press the Digital Touch button, and then use motions to transmit:
   - To transmit a single tap or a series of taps, just tap the screen.

- To "kiss" on an electronic device, you must tap the screen with two fingers. Put down the phone and send.
- Put two fingers on the screen where your heart is beating and the rhythm will be animated on the screen.
- Feel your heartbeat with two fingers on the screen, then drag it down to transmit.
- Fireball: Keep one finger on the screen until a flame appears. Rise to transmit.

Expose Your Whereabouts

Scroll down and choose Send Location to send a link to a map of your present location to someone.

Make sure Share My Location is enabled in Settings > [your name] > Find My > Share My Location on your associated iPhone. Alternatively, you may enable Share My Location on your cellular Apple Watch by opening the Settings app, and navigating to Privacy > Location Services.

Share your location in a message.

A map pinpointing the sender's location appears on the messages screen.

Get in touch with the recipient of your message.

1. To see more of a discussion, scroll down the page.
2. After selecting Details, choose a communication method from the menu that appears, such as Phone, Message, Mail, or Walkie-Talkie.

To send the contact to others, scroll down and press the Share Contact button.

USE YOUR WATCH TO RESPOND TO MESSAGES

Get Back To Someone

Scroll down the message by rotating the Digital Crown, and then choose a response option.

By touching and holding a message in a chat, you may instantly answer with a Tapback, such as thumbs up or a heart.

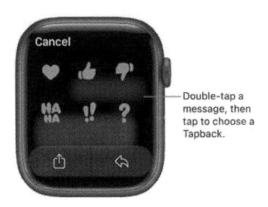

Double-tap a message, then tap to choose a Tapback.

A Tapback discussion in Messages with the choices of a heart, thumbs up, thumbs down, Ha Ha,!! and?. A comment section follows.

Make A Direct Response
Make a direct response to a single post in a thread.

You can help keep things structured in a group chat by replying to individual messages right in the thread.

1. To respond to a particular message in a Messages thread, touch and hold the message in question.
2. Reply by typing your thoughts into the reply box and hitting the Send button.

The recipient of your reply will be the only one to read it.

Spread The Word

The Messages app's Sharing screen displays a conversation between two friends.

Messages from friends often include insights and feelings that you want to share. Here's what you need to do to get your point across:

1. Touch and hold a message in a chat, and then hit the Share button.
2. Select the contacts you most often communicate with or go straight to Messages or Mail.
3. Select Messages or Mail, and then add recipients and a subject line if you're sending an email.
4. Just hit the send button.

EXAMINE THE FORECAST

Siri, on your Apple Watch, can tell you the forecast: Get tomorrow's Honolulu forecast by asking a question like "What's the forecast like?"

See What The Weather's Like

- Check out today's weather and conditions: Launch the Apple Watch's weather app. Select a city and use your finger to swipe through the hourly weather, condition, and temperature predictions.

The hourly forecast on the Weather app.

- Check out the 10-day forecast and details on the air quality, UV index, wind speed, humidity, and visibility: Select an area by tapping on it, then scrolling down.

  To go back to the city list, tap the up arrow in the upper left corner.

Two cities' weather information is shown in a list format inside the Weather app.

Not all areas have access to air quality reports.

Put In A Town

1. Launch the Apple Watch's weather app.
2. Select Add City from the bottom of the list of cities.
3. The name of the city must be typed in (only compatible with Apple Watch Series 7 and Apple Watch Series 9) or spoken into (only compatible with Apple Watch Series 9).

   On the Series 7 and Series 9 Apple Watches, you can access Scribble by swiping up from the bottom of the display and then selecting the app.

4. Select the city from the list that appears once you press Search.

The cities you add to the Apple Watch's Weather app will appear on your iPhone in the same sequence.

Drop A City

1. Launch the Apple Watch's weather app.
2. To delete a city from the list, slide it to the left and then hit the X.

Modify Weather Records

You may customize the list of cities shown in the Weather app by selecting a different measure to show for each location.

1. Get out your Apple Watch and check the forecast.
2. Select Viewing from the menu bar.
3. Pick the Temperature, the Precipitation, or the Conditions.

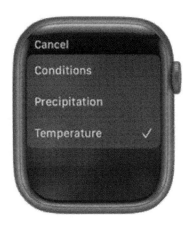

Conditions, Precipitation, and Temperature are the three options shown by the Weather app.

Pick your starting town
1. Launch the Apple Watch's Settings menu.
2. Select Weather, then tap Default City, and then select a location from the list you've created.

On the iPhone app for the Apple Watch, choose My Watch > Weather > Default City.

If you've set your watch to display the local weather, you can see what's happening there.

Observe Any Weather Updates

The Weather app has issued a warning about possible dangers at the beach.

A warning may flash at the top of the Weather app when a major weather event is forecast. Tap Learn More for further information on the gathering.

CHECK OUT A FRIEND'S WHEREABOUTS

Check out a friend's whereabouts on your Apple Watch.

Using the Find People app, you can easily track down the people that matter to you and let them know where you are. When friends and relatives with an iPhone, iPad, iPod touch, Apple Watch Series 4 or later share their positions with you, you may see them all at once on a map. You may choose to get notified when certain areas are entered or left by friends and relatives.

Your profile in Find People, complete with a "Share My Location" button.

Add A Friend

1. Launch the Apple Watch's Find People app.

2. Scroll down and choose the Share My Location option.
3. Select a contact by tapping the Dictation, Contacts, or Keypad buttons.
4. Choose an available contact method (email or phone).
5. Make your location public for an hour, the rest of the day, or forever.

When you share your location with a buddy, they will be alerted. They are free to tell you where they are if they so want. Once your buddy has permitted you to track their position, you can use the Find My app on your iPhone, iPad, iPod touch, or Mac, or the Find People app on your Apple Watch to see exactly where they are at any given time.

On the Find People screen, hit the contact's name, and then tap Stop Sharing to terminate location sharing.

If you don't want your Apple Watch to broadcast your whereabouts to the world, open the Settings app, go to Privacy & Security > Location Services, and off Share My Location.

Locate Your Pals And Hang Around
1. When you launch the Find People app on your Apple Watch, you'll be presented with a list of

your friends, along with an estimate of how far away from you they currently are. To see more friends, just rotate the Digital Crown.

2. If you tap a friend's name, you'll be taken to a map showing their general position.

3. You may access your buddy list by tapping in the upper left corner.

A window containing two entries, one for you and one for the other person whose location you've provided.

You may also consult Siri. Just ask, "Where is Julie?"

If your buddy has an Apple Watch that supports cellular and is sharing their location but has forgotten to bring their iPhone, the Apple Watch will still be able to monitor their whereabouts.

Share your travel plans with a buddy

1. Launch the Apple Watch's Find People app.
2. Select the contact you want to notify, then scroll down and hit the Notify button.
3. On the next page, choose Notify [name of buddy] to let them know when you've left or arrived at a place.

Find out where your buddy is at any given time

1. Launch the Apple Watch's Find People app.
2. To send a notification to a friend, touch on them, then on Notify Me.
3. To get alerts when a buddy departs or arrives at their location, use the Notify Me feature.

LOOK FOR INSTRUCTIONS USING YOUR WATCH

You may call a buddy or look for instructions using your Apple Watch.

Get directions to a buddy fast using Find People.

Find Your Pal's Whereabouts

- Launch the Apple Watch's Find People app.
- Simply launch the Maps app by tapping your buddy, scrolling down, and then tapping Directions.

- If you tap the route, it will take you from where you are right now to where your buddy is.

Reach Out To A Friend

1. Launch the Apple Watch's Find People app.
2. You may phone, email, or send a message to a friend by tapping them, scrolling down, and tapping the Contact button.

TRACK YOUR LOST DEVICE
The watch may be used to track lost gadgets.

If you've misplaced an Apple device, you may use the Apple Watch's Find Devices app to track it down. You need to link your Apple gadgets to your Apple ID before you can locate them.

Two gadgets, an Apple Watch and a pair of AirPods, are shown in the Find gadgets app.

Track The Precise Position Of A Gadget

The Find Devices app will show you exactly where your internet device is. While used with a compatible device, Find Devices can pinpoint its location even while the gadget is dormant, in Low Power Mode, or airplane mode.

Select a gadget using the Apple Watch's Find app.

- The device's location, if known, will be shown on a map. Above the map, you'll see details like the device's current charge, its last known location, and how long it's been since it connected to Wi-Fi or a cellular network. A rough pinpoint is shown below the map.
- If there is no known location for the device, the words "No location" will appear next to the item's name. Select Notify when Found from the Notifications menu. Once it has been found, you will be notified.

Make A Noise On Your Apple Device

Make a noise on your Apple device (phone, tablet, Mac, or smartwatch).

1. Select a gadget using the Apple Watch's Find app.
2. Select the Sound Play button.
   - Is the gadget connected to the internet? After a brief pause, a sound begins and, over two

minutes, the level steadily rises until finally peaking. If it has such capability, the gadget vibrates. The gadget displays a "Find My" message.
The email address associated with your Apple ID will also get a confirmation message.

- If the gadget is not online, you'll see "Sound Pending." This will trigger the sound the next time the device connects to a cellular or Wi-Fi network.

Put On Your Headphones
Put on your headphones, whether they are AirPods or Beats, and play a sound.

Use the Find Devices feature on your Apple Watch to send a sound to your AirPods or Beats headphones.

If you have a compatible model of AirPods, you can even use the case to listen to a sound via headphones.

1. Select a gadget using the Apple Watch's Find app.
2. Select the Sound Play button. If you have lost one of your AirPods or AirPods Pro, you may silence it by searching for it using the Left and Right buttons.

- If connected to the internet, the gadget will instantly begin playing a sound for two minutes.
  The email address associated with your Apple ID will also get a confirmation message.
- If the gadget isn't connected to the internet, your Apple Watch will alert you the next time it's within range.

Find Your Way To A Gadget

The Apple Watch's Maps software may be used to acquire driving instructions to a device's current location.

1. To get instructions for a specific device, launch the Find Devices app on your Apple Watch and then touch it.
2. Select the Directions button to launch Maps.
3. If you tap the route, it will take you from where you are right now to where the gadget is.

Find out immediately whether you've forgotten to take anything with you.

Whenever you leave your smartphone behind, you can get a notice so you don't lose it. You may also designate some areas as "Trusted Locations" where your device will not trigger an alarm.

1. Launch the Apple Watch's Find My Devices app.
2. Select the gadget you'd want to alert on by tapping its name.
3. To activate Notify When Left Behind, hit the button located underneath Notifications.

To set up a notice when your iPhone is left behind, open the Find My app, go to Devices, select the device in question, and then hit Notify When Left Behind. To get alerts when you are left behind, activate the feature and follow the on-screen prompts.

To add a trusted place, pick a recommended place from the drop-down menu or touch New area, go to the desired area using the map, and finally, hit Done.

Declare A Gadget Missing

If you lose your iPhone, iPad, iPod touch, or Apple Watch, or if your Mac is stolen, you may activate Lost Mode or lock it.

1. Select a gadget using the Apple Watch's Find app.
2. Select "Lost Mode" from the menu and activate it.

What happens when you report a gadget lost:

- Your Apple ID will get a confirmation email.

- The Lock Screen displays a notification saying the device has been misplaced and providing contact information.
- There are no visual or audible indicators for incoming messages, notifications, or alarms on your smartphone. You can still get the phone and FaceTime calls on your gadget.
- This device cannot use Apple Pay at this time. Your Apple Pay information, along with your student ID and Express Transit cards, will be deleted. Even if your device isn't online, your credit, debit, and student ID cards will be canceled. When your device reconnects to the internet, any remaining Express Transit cards will be deleted.
- Your present position and any location changes are shown on a map for your iPhone, iPad, iPod touch, or Apple Watch.

USE AIRTAG TO TRACK A MISPLACED ITEM

Use Find Items to track down a misplaced AirTag or anything else.

If you've registered an AirTag or third-party item to your Apple ID and then misplaced it, you may use the Find Items app on your Apple Watch to track it down.

A set of keys with an AirTag connected to them may be located using the Find Items app.

Find out where something is stored

Launch the Find Items app on your Apple Watch, and then choose the object you want to track down.

- If it's possible to track down the object, you'll be able to view its location on the map. Above the map, you'll see details like the device's current charge, its last known location, and how long it's been since it connected to Wi-Fi or a cellular network. A rough pinpoint is shown below the map.
- If the object can't be found, the last known location and time will be shown. Select Notify

When Found from the Notifications menu. As soon as it's found again, you'll be notified.

Put On A Tune

You can use a sound to locate an object if it is close by.

The Play Sound button won't appear if the item doesn't support playing sounds.

1. To assign a sound to an item, launch the Find Items app on your Apple Watch and touch the object in question.
2. Select the Sound Play button.

   You may interrupt the sound's playback by selecting Stop Sound before it finishes automatically.

How To Go Somewhere Specific

Using the Apple Watch's Maps app, you may find your way to an item's last known location or its present position.

1. Tap the object you need instructions to on your Apple Watch's Find Items app's main screen.
2. Select the Directions button to launch Maps.
3. If you tap the route, it will show you how to travel from where you are right now to where the item is kept.

Find out right away whether you've forgotten anything

You may get an alert if you've forgotten to take an item with you. In addition, you may designate certain areas as "Trusted Locations," or spots where you can leave your item without worrying about being notified.

1. Launch the Apple Watch's Find App.
2. Select the content you want to get alerts for by tapping on it.
3. Select the "Notify When Left Behind" option and toggle it on.

To do this, launch the Find My app on your iPhone, choose Items, touch the item for which you'd want to get alerts, and finally select Notify When Left Behind. To get alerts when you are left behind, activate the feature and follow the on-screen prompts.

To add a trusted place, pick a recommended place from the drop-down menu or touch a new area, go to the desired area using the map, and finally, hit Done.

DECLARE A GADGET MISSING

Use Apple Watch's Find Items feature to report a misplaced AirTag or other item.

Use the Find Items app to report a missing AirTag or third-party item associated with your Apple ID.

1. Select an item and launch the Find It app on your Apple Watch.
2. Select "Lost Mode" from the menu and activate it.

You may share information about your object with whoever discovers it by having them connect to it.

Disable The Lost Mode On A Certain Item

If you locate what you were looking for, you may off Lost Mode.

1. Tap the object, and then launch the Find Items app on your Apple Watch.
2. Select Lost Mode, and then select Off to disable it.

CHAPTER SEVEN

HOW TO USE WATCH'S CYCLE TRACKING

Keep track of your menstrual cycle with the help of the Cycle Tracking app. You may track symptoms like aches and pains, as well as add flow data. The Cycle Tracking app may send you notifications when it determines that your next period or fertile window is about to begin based on the data you've entered. Your heart rate data may be used in conjunction with your recorded information to further refine Cycle Tracking's predictions. Wearing an Apple Watch Series 9 to bed each night may help the app better forecast your menstruation and offer historical ovulation estimations based on your wrist's temperature.

Please be assured that your privacy will be respected and your preferences respected while using the Health app.

Commence Tracking Cycles

1. Launch the iPhone's Health application.
2. To see the Health Categories screen, tap Browse in the app's upper right corner.

3. Input Cycle Tracking.
4. To begin customizing your alerts and other settings, choose Get Started.

Open the Health app on your iPhone, touch Browse, tap Cycle Tracking, and then tap Options next to Cycle Log to make any necessary changes once you've set up Cycle Tracking.

Watch Cycle Tracking

1. Launch the iPhone's Cycle Tracking app.
2. Select the choices that apply to your period by tapping the buttons, such as the flow level and symptoms you're experiencing.

Your input is recorded in the iPhone's Cycle log. Using the iPhone's Health app, you can enable alerts for things like imminent periods, fertile window forecasts, and, on Apple Watch Series 9, retroactive ovulation estimations, all of which will be sent to your wrist through push notifications.

Watch the display for the "Cycle Tracking" feature.

You may keep track of things like pregnancy, breastfeeding, and contraception usage, as well as other lifestyle choices, in the iPhone's Health app. Period forecasts, fertile window predictions, and Apple Watch Series 9 retrospective ovulation estimations may all be disabled in settings.

You should not use the Cycle Tracking app as a contraceptive. You shouldn't use information gathered by the Cycle Tracking app to make medical decisions.

GET HISTORICAL ESTIMATIONS WITH YOUR WATCH

With Watch Series 9, you can get historical estimations of when you ovulated.

If you wear your Apple Watch Series 9 to bed every night, it will record your body temperature during the night and utilize that information to improve its period prediction and retrospective ovulation estimation algorithms (*not available in all areas).

You should not use the Cycle Tracking app as a contraceptive. You shouldn't use information gathered by the Cycle Tracking app to make medical decisions.

Start Recording Your Wrist's Temperature
1. Create a Sleep and Cycle Log.
2. Wear your Apple Watch while you sleep with the Sleep Focus on to get an accurate temperature reading.

   After five nights, the data from the wrist thermometers will be ready.

3. In the Health app on your iPhone, choose Wrist Temperature under Body Measurements after selecting Browse.

After two cycles of sleeping with your Apple Watch on, the device should be able to provide an estimate of when you last ovulated.

Your body temperature varies naturally and might change from one night to the next for a variety of reasons. Environmental variables, such as the temperature of the room in which you sleep, may also affect wrist temperature.

Cycle Tracking Wrist Temperature Off

1. The iPhone's Health app may be accessed through the Browse button followed by the Cycle Tracking option.
2. Select Settings, and then disable the Use Wrist Temperature option.

If you choose to disable monitoring of your wrist temperature, you will no longer obtain historical ovulation estimations, and your period forecasts will not be based on your wrist temperature data.

MANAGE YOUR HOME

The Apple Watch Home app displays a light fixture that can be controlled from your wrist. The volume is at 90% and there is a Done button in the upper left corner.

The Home app offers a safe method of managing HomeKit-enabled devices including lamps, door locks, televisions, climate controls, blinds, and plugs. On compatible devices, you can also communicate through Intercom and see live footage from HomeKit Secure Video cameras. Everything you need to use your Apple Watch is conveniently located on your wrist.

When you use the Home app on your iPhone for the first time, the setup assistant guides you through the process of making a house. Then you can set up scenarios by defining rooms and adding HomeKit-enabled devices. Your Apple Watch can access the accessories, scenarios, and rooms you've added to your iPhone.

Say something to Siri like, "Turn off the lights in the office."

Check The Current Condition Of Your House
The Home app updates you on the current state of your connected devices, such as the thermostat's temperature reading or the door's unlock status. Accessory management and background info are only a touch away.

1. Launch the Apple Watch's Home app.

2. Select one of the round icons that appear under your address.

The Home app with the accessory on top and the status icons at the bottom.

When a status displays several accessories, touching the status allows you to manage each accessory or group of accessories. If all the lights in the living room and bedroom are on, for instance, tapping the status will allow you to switch off just the lights in the living room.

Manage The Setup Of Smart Home Features
When you open the Home app on your Apple Watch, the most important scenes and accessories will always be shown at the top. For instance, you may have a coffee maker in the morning and a bedroom light in the evening.

To access the remainder of your add-ons, swipe up and choose Cameras, Favorites, or a specific room.

The Home app display of a room list with two rooms and a camera.

Any of the following may be used to manage a peripheral:

- Activate or deactivate a feature: You can turn on a light or open a door with a house key by tapping the attachment.
- Modify the settings of a gadget: To accessorize your device, click the More icon. Select "Done" to get back to the toolset.

  Accessory-specific controls may be found. Some light bulbs, for instance, allow you to adjust the light intensity in addition to the color temperature. More options may be accessed by swiping to the left.

- Manage a variety of interior accents, including personal favorites: To modify an item's settings, choose it from Favorites or a specific area, and then either touch its name or the More button.
- See what's being captured by a camera: Select Cameras, and then a specific camera.

Launch a scene from your Apple Watch by opening the Home app and tapping the scene you want to use.

Check Out The Other House
If you have more than one house connected to your Apple Watch, you may switch between them with ease.

You may perform any of the following after you've launched the Home app on your Apple Watch:

- Tap the home icon if the Home Screen is visible.
- If a certain house is currently shown, you may switch to another by tapping.

Communication Through Intercom
Send an Intercom message to your household using the Apple Watch's Home app. Room or zone-specific Intercom transmissions are also possible.

1. Launch the Watch's Home app.

2. To use the intercom, swipe down and then hit the button.
3. To illustrate this point, try asking, "Who ate the last piece of pizza?"
4. Select the End button.

All the HomePod speakers in your house, as well as the iOS, iPadOS, and watchOS devices of everyone in your home who can send and receive Intercom messages, will get a recording of your voice.

Just lift your Apple Watch and say something like, "Hey Siri, tell the office 'The movie is starting'" or "Hey Siri, announce upstairs 'I'm going to the store'" to send a message to a HomePod in a specified room or zone.

CONTROL YOUR SMART HOME GADGETS

Control your smart home gadgets from your Watch.

HomeKit-enabled devices may be controlled from afar using an iPhone and an Apple Watch that is synced to an Apple TV (3rd generation or later) or HomePod. The Apple TV or HomePod may serve as a hub for your smart home, allowing you to control and interact with your devices from afar.

Embrace Distal Access

You may activate Home by going to your iPhone's Settings > [your name] > iCloud. Make sure that the same Apple ID is being used across all of your devices.

The Apple TV will automatically link with your iPhone if you use the same Apple ID on both devices.

SKIM ARTICLES ON YOUR WATCH

The Apple Watch's News app keeps you abreast of the latest headlines and displays articles tailored to your interests.

The News app is not yet accessible in all areas or countries.

Try out the News app for some reading material.

Multiple formats exist for reading news articles:

- Launch the Apple Watch's News app.
- Select the watch face's "News" complication.
- Select an article of interest from the Siri watch face by touching it.
- Select a breaking story alert in News.

Spend Some Time With A News Article

1. Launch the Apple Watch's News app.
2. Turning the Digital Crown will advance you through the plot description.
3. Scroll down to the bottom of the page and click Save for Later to read it on your iPhone, iPad, or Mac at a later time.
4. Follow one of these steps to read the article on your mobile device:
   - For the iPhone, launch the News app, choose Following, tap Saved Stories, and then select the desired article.
   - If you're using an iPad, launch the News app, then hit Saved Stories in the left column.
   - On a Mac, launch the News app, go to Saved Stories using the app's sidebar, and click the story.

Open the Settings app on your iPhone, choose News, and then toggle Restrict news in Today to view just news from the channels you follow.

When you restrict stories, fewer stories will display in Today and the other feeds. If you choose to follow just one entertainment-related channel, for instance, that channel's posts will be the only ones included in your Entertainment topic feed.

Restricting stories will hide the Top Stories and Trending Stories sections.

Navigate To The Next Or Previous News Item
1. Launch the Apple Watch's News app.
2. If there is more to read, swipe to the left.
3. Just swipe right to go back a story.

After reading the summary, go to the next article by tapping Next Story at the very bottom of the page.

Launch News Articles
1. Launch the Apple Watch's News app.
2. Turn on iPhone and launch the multitasking menu. (Swipe up from the bottom edge and stop on an iPhone with Face ID; double-click the Home button on an older iPhone.)
3. Simply open News by tapping the button that displays at the bottom of the screen.

ACTIVATE VOICEOVER WITH YOUR WATCH

Apple Watch users, activate VoiceOver!

Using VoiceOver, you may operate your Apple Watch without being able to view the screen. Navigate the interface with easy motions while VoiceOver reads out your choices.

Adjust The Volume Of Voiceover

1. Launch the Apple Watch's Settings menu.
2. To activate VoiceOver, choose Accessibility > VoiceOver from the menu.

   If you want to disable VoiceOver, just double-tap the button.

   Command Siri, "Turn VoiceOver on" or "Turn VoiceOver off."

Open the Apple Watch app on your iPhone, choose My Watch, go to Accessibility, and then select the VoiceOver option to activate it for your Apple Watch. Additionally, you may use the Accessibility Shortcut.

Installing Voiceover

If you triple-click the Digital Crown when setting up your Apple Watch, VoiceOver will provide guidance.

Signals For The Voiceover Interface

If you're using VoiceOver on your Apple Watch, you can operate it using these movements.

VoiceOver is compatible with Always On Displays. When you tap the screen when it's dark, VoiceOver will zero in on whatever you tapped.

- Look around the screen! You may hear the item's name read out as you move your finger over the screen. One finger tapping will choose the object, and one finger swiping to the left or right will select the item next to it. Using two fingers, you may swipe left, right, up, or down to navigate between pages.
- Using two fingers draw a "z" shape on the screen to return to the previous screen if you find yourself on a route you didn't want to go.
- To take action, double-tap an item instead of tapping it once if you have VoiceOver enabled. This works for opening apps, toggling options, and so on. Tap or swipe to the desired app icon, list item, or option switch, and then double-tap to activate it. To deactivate VoiceOver, double-tap anywhere on the screen after tapping the VoiceOver button.
- Take the following extra steps: Listen for the phrase "actions available" when you hover over an object that allows for more than one action. Double-tap to carry out an action selected with a swipe up or down.
- VoiceOver may be paused while reading by tapping the screen with two fingers. Use two fingers to tap again to continue.

- Double-tap and hold with two fingers, then drag up or down to adjust the VoiceOver volume. Alternatively, you may use VoiceOver by opening the Apple Watch app on your iPhone, tapping My Watch, and then tapping Accessibility > VoiceOver.

Put The Voiceover Dial To Use

The rotor allows you to quickly navigate between on-screen options and alter VoiceOver preferences. Words, characters, actions, headings, volume, and speaking rate may all be adjusted using the Apple Watch's rotor.

To adjust the volume of VoiceOver, use two fingers to spin the screen like a dial. The rotor speed is announced by voiceover. Keep turning your fingers to listen to different options. As soon as you hear the desired setting, you may stop spinning your fingers.

To use the rotor, mimic these hand motions.

Action	Gesture
Choose a rotor setting	Rotate two fingers
Move to the previous item or increase (depending on the rotor setting)	Swipe up
Move to the next item or decrease (depending on the rotor setting)	Swipe down

Set Preferences For Voiceover

The Apple Watch may be used to make changes to VoiceOver's actions. To enable VoiceOver on your Apple Watch, open the Settings app and go to Accessibility > VoiceOver.

- Disable VoiceOver.
- Slow down or speed up your voice.
- Level up your VoiceOver!
- Toggle Speech Settings
- Select Speech, and then tweak the voice, pitch, and rotor language settings as needed.
- Toggle the use of haptics
- Change to Braille settings

  Select Braille and tweak settings for Braille output and input as well as word wrap, alert display time, and Braille tables.

- Options for Keyboards (Series 7 and Series 9 Apple Watches)

  Once you've paired your Bluetooth keyboard with your Apple Watch, you can customize its sound effects, typing feedback, modifier keys, how long it takes to type, and more by going to Settings > Keyboards.

- To disable VoiceOver suggestions,
- Use the Digital Crown for navigation.
- Raise your hand if you want to hear what's being emphasized.
- To protect your privacy when using VoiceOver, use Screen Curtain.
- Minutes of silence
- Setup Gesture Hands

Your iPhone also has access to the same settings. Launch Apple Watch, choose My Watch, and then go to Accessibility > VoiceOver in the app's settings menu.

USE VOICEOVER FOR WATCH SETUP

The Apple Watch and iPhone pairing process is simplified with VoiceOver's assistance. To activate VoiceOver, touch and hold the screen while swiping your finger left or right. The highlighted object may be activated with a double tap.

Use Voiceover For Watch Setup

1. To activate your Apple Watch, press and hold the side button (located below the Digital Crown) for a few seconds.
2. To activate VoiceOver on your Apple Watch, just triple-click the Digital Crown.
3. Get your iPhone within range of your Apple Watch.
4. Double-tap Continue on your iPhone to proceed.
5. Double-tap the "Set Up Apple Watch" icon on your iPhone.
6. Automatic pairing may be tried by pointing the iPhone camera at the watch from a distance of roughly 6 inches.

   If you hear a confirmation tone, it means the pairing has been successful. Manual pairing is an option if you're having trouble; just repeat steps 7-13.

7. To manually pair your iPhone with your Apple Watch, double-tap the Watch icon.
8. To access the Info menu, double-tap the Digital Crown on your Apple Watch.
9. Choose your Apple Watch ID from the menu at the top of the screen. You overhear your Apple

Watch's identification, which sounds like "Apple Watch 52345" or something similar.

10. Double-tap this identical identifier on your iPhone to select it.
11. To hear the six-digit pairing code, choose the option to do so on your Apple Watch.
12. Use the iPhone's keyboard to enter the pairing code shown on your Apple Watch.

The connection is successful; you will get a tap from Apple Watch and the message "Your Apple Watch is paired." Tap the notifications to reply if pairing fails. You may try again when your Apple Watch and iPhone app are reset.

13. Double-tap the Apple Watch app on your iPhone, and then choose either Restore from Backup or Set Up as New.
14. To proceed with setting up your Apple Watch, just listen to the voice instructions.

After the initial setup is complete, Apple Watch will automatically sync with your iPhone. The iPhone's Sync Progress button may be used to monitor the process. After hearing "sync complete," you may begin using your Apple Watch, which will then show the appropriate time. Simply swipe left or right to see several options for the watch face.

Use Your iPhone To Manage Your Watch

It may be simpler for those with mobility or sensory impairments to use the iPhone's bigger display to interact with their Apple Watch. Inputs other than touching the Apple Watch display, such as voice commands, sound actions, head tracking, or external Made for iPhone switches, are all viable options thanks to Apple Watch Mirroring and the accessibility capabilities of the iPhone.

Mirroring on Apple Watch is supported by Series 6, Series 7, and Series 9 models.

1. It's time to get into the iPhone's settings.
2. To activate Apple Watch Mirroring, go to Settings, then Accessibility.

The screen of your iPhone will look like the one on your Apple Watch. The reflection may be used for gesturing.

- Swipe the screen up or down to scroll.
- Use a left or right swipe motion to move between displays.
- Tap the Digital Crown to use it as a button.
- Aside from button press reveals: To use the side button, tap the screen.
- Tap and hold the Digital Crown on the screen to activate Siri.

Your Watch Can Manage Adjacent Electronics

If you have an Apple Watch and an iPhone, your Apple Watch can also operate your iPhone or iPad.

1. Launch the Apple Watch's Settings menu.
2. To manage nearby devices, choose the Accessibility menu.

   Your iOS device and the computer must both have the same Apple ID and be connected to the same Wi-Fi network.

3. Pick a gadget. If there is more than one nearby, you should use the button.

   The buttons have the same functions as the ones on your smartphone.

   - Home Menu
   - Free App Swapper
   - Message Dispensing Hub
   - Administration Hub
   - Siri
   - Options (with gesture controls for playing media and other personalization options)

If you have VoiceOver enabled on your Apple Watch and you want to use it to command a nearby device,

VoiceOver on that device will also be activated, and the motions you make using VoiceOver on your Apple Watch will be carried out on the device.

Switch Control buttons (such as Move, Next, and Select) display on your watch when the feature is activated on a nearby device.

APPLY WATCH'S ASSISTIVE TOUCH FEATURE

If you have trouble touching the screen or tapping the buttons on your Apple Watch, AssistiveTouch may assist. Built-in sensors on the Apple Watch allow you to do a variety of tasks by just waving your hand.

You can use AssistiveTouch gestures to do the following and more:

- Input taps the screen
- To use the Digital Crown, just press and turn it.
- Slide between windows on your mobile device.
- Maintain pressure on the side button
- Connect to the Dock, Notification Center, and Control Center
- Expose software
- Utilize Apple Pay
- Double-clicking the side button is confirmed.

- Put Siri to work!
- Put Siri to work for you

Put Assistive Touch In Place

1. Launch the Apple Watch's Settings menu.
2. Turn on AssistiveTouch by selecting Options > Accessibility > AssistiveTouch.
3. Select Hand Gestures from the menu and toggle it on.

   Press "Learn more" underneath the Hand Gestures switch, and then tap each motion, to find out how to utilize them. When you touch a gesture, a live-action video guides you through the motions step by step.

To activate AssistiveTouch, launch the Apple Watch app on your iPhone, go to My Watch, hit Accessibility, and finally tap AssistiveTouch.

Assistive Touch Is Compatible With Watch

You can use the following hand gestures to control your Apple Watch if you have AssistiveTouch and Hand Gestures enabled:

- Squeeze: in advance
- Back and forward pinching
- Tap: Clench
- Press and hold for the Quick Menu

Here's how you could, with the Meridian watch face up, utilize AssistiveTouch with the Weather app:

1. AssistiveTouch may be activated with a double clench.

   The Calendar complications are highlighted.

2. To access the Temperature challenge, pinch and clench until you reach it.
3. Clench once when the Weather app launches to switch between temperature and forecast.
4. To see the UV Index, squeeze the screen once and then again to scroll down to "Air Quality."
5. To return to Air Quality, just double-tap the screen.
6. The Action Menu may be accessed via a double clinch.

   You may pinch to advance through the activities and double-pinch to rewind.

7. Clench the crown once to choose the Press Crown action and return to the watch face.

Make Use Of The Moving Pointer

The Motion Pointer on the Apple Watch allows you to interact with the device in a variety of ways, including by tilting the watch up and down and side to side in addition to pinching and clenching. For instance, here's how to utilize the Motion Pointer to go about the Activity app:

1. If you double-clench your Apple Watch when it is in list view with the watch face visible, you may use AssistiveTouch.
2. Clench twice more to bring up the Action Menu, pinch to scroll to the Press Crown entry, then clench to act.
3. Clench to launch the Activity app if it isn't previously chosen with a pinch or double pinch.
4. To access the Interaction action, double-clench to bring up the Action Menu, then pinch to pick it.

   Choose the moving pointer.

5. The Motion Pointer may be activated by clenching.

   The screen now displays a cursor.

6. You may scroll down the screen by tilting your watch so that the pointer is at the bottom. The Sharing screen may be accessed by swiping in from the right side of the screen.
7. Just hover the mouse over the button you want to tap for a few seconds.
8. If you double-click the crown, the Action Menu appears; squeeze to pick Press Crown; then

double-click the crown again to return to the watch face.

Take Prompt Action

When an alert appears on your Apple Watch, you may quickly take action to deal with it. A notification may appear, for instance, to inform you that you may double-pinch to answer an incoming call. In addition to starting a workout when Apple Watch detects exercise-like behavior, pausing an alarm, or stopping a timer, fast actions may now be used to snap a picture when the Camera app's viewfinder and shutter button are shown. Here's how to toggle rapid actions on and off.

1. Launch the Apple Watch's Settings menu.
2. Select an item under the Accessibility > Quick Actions menu.

Quick actions may be toggled on and off, made accessible just when AssistiveTouch is active, or disabled altogether. The action button may be emphasized with or without a banner, depending on whether you choose the Full or Minimal design.

For further experience with the fast actions gesture, try tapping "Try it out."

Modify Your Assistive Touch Settings

The Motion Pointer's sensitivity may be adjusted, and its pinch and clench movements can be given new functions.

Accessibility > AssistiveTouch may be found in the Settings menu of your Apple Watch.

- Select Hand Gestures, then select a gesture, and then select an action or Siri shortcut to personalize gestures.
- Change the Motion Pointer's sensitivity, activation time, movement tolerance, and hot edges by tapping the Motion Pointer icon.
- You may choose between two distinct scanning modes: Automatic, in which activities are highlighted sequentially, and Manual, in which you must manually highlight each action before proceeding to the next.
- Appearance-wise, you may make the highlight stand out more by activating High Contrast. You may change the highlight color by tapping the Color button.
- You may personalize the menu by adding your preferred actions, moving and resizing the Action Menu, and modifying the auto-scroll speed.
- AssistiveTouch confirmation: When enabled, AssistiveTouch will be used whenever a double-

click of the side button is necessary, even when paying with a password.

Accessibility > AssistiveTouch may also be accessed via the Apple Watch app on the iPhone by selecting My Watch > Accessibility > AssistiveTouch.

CHAPTER EIGHT

HOW TO ZOOM IN ON YOUR WATCH

Zoom in on the Apple Watch screen to see more detail.

Activate Zoom

1. To activate Zoom, launch the Apple Watch's Settings menu.
2. Accessibility > Zoom to activate.

Zoom may also be activated from the iPhone by opening the Apple Watch app, selecting My Watch, tapping Accessibility, and finally selecting Zoom.

Powering The Magnifier

You can use your Apple Watch to do these things after you've activated Zoom.

- Double-tap the screen with two fingers to zoom in or out on your Apple Watch.

  If you want a closer look while you're setting up your Apple Watch, try double-tapping with two fingers.

- To pan the view, just use two fingers to drag the screen. By rotating the Digital Crown, you may scroll the whole page, both horizontally and vertically. You can see where you are on the page by clicking the little Zoom button that displays.
- To toggle between using the Digital Crown to pan and using the Digital Crown in its usual, non-Zoom mode (to, say, scroll a list or zoom a map), tap the display once with two fingers.
- Change the zoom level: Drag your fingers up or down the screen by double-tapping and holding them there. Adjust the maximum zoom level by using the plus or minus button.

The Watch's Haptic Feedback
Watch's haptic feedback makes it easy to tell time.

Apple Watch can silently display the time by tapping out the hours, minutes, and seconds on the wearer's wrist. Proceed as follows:

1. Launch the Apple Watch's Settings menu.
2. Select Taptic Time by selecting Clock and then scrolling down.
3. Taptic Time may be activated and any one of three modes (Digits, Terse, or Morse Code)

selected. Time is denoted as follows, in both hours and minutes:

- Apple Watch long taps every 10 hours, short taps every hour after that, long taps every 10 minutes, and short touches every minute after that to display the time in 10-minute increments.
- Sparse: every five hours, your Apple Watch will make a lengthy tap, then every hour and a quarter will make a small tap.
- The Apple Watch displays the time in Morse code by tapping out each numeral.

4. A haptic representation of the time may be felt by touching and holding two fingers on the watch's face.

When the Always On Display is off, Taptic Time continues to function normally.

Taptic Time on the iPhone may also be customized. To activate Taptic Time, launch the Apple Watch app on your iPhone, choose My Watch, then Clock > Taptic Time.

If you have Apple Watch configured to always speak the time, Taptic Time will not work. Taptic Time requires that Control With Silent Mode be enabled in Settings > Clock > Speak Time before it can be used.

MODIFY THE WATCH'S DISPLAY FONT SIZE

Modify the Apple Watch's display by changing the font size and other options.

It is possible to change the size of the text and other parameters to facilitate the use of the interface.

Modify The Font Size

1. To do this, touch and hold the screen's bottom, then swipe up.
2. Use the Digital Crown to make the text larger or smaller by tapping the Adjust Text Size button.

Customize The Appearance Of Text

The ability to customize the appearance of text and other elements

Various settings allow you to alter the visual presentation of on-screen elements, such as the ability to make text bold or switch to grayscale. You may toggle the following features on or off in the Accessibility section of the Settings app on your Apple Watch.

• Switchable Labels

To have a more comprehensive understanding of your location, toggle button labels on. When labels are enabled, you will see a one (1) next to each enabled option and a zero (0) next to each disabled one.

- Grayscale
- Limit openness

When used against certain backdrops, a decrease in transparency improves readability.

- Italicized words

Alternatively, you may access the Apple Watch settings from the iPhone app by going to Watch > My Watch > Accessibility.

Restarting your Apple Watch may be required for the bold and grayscale adjustments to take effect.

Animate Less

The Home Screen and app transitions may be slowed down to a crawl.

1. Launch the Apple Watch's Settings menu.
2. To enable Reduce Motion, go to Accessibility > Reduce Motion.

To activate Reduce Motion, launch the Apple Watch app on your iPhone and go to My Watch > Accessibility > Reduce Motion.

In grid mode on the Home Screen, all app icons will be the same size as soon as you activate Reduce Motion.

Adjust The Rate With The Button On The Side

1. Launch the Apple Watch's Settings menu.
2. Choose the Side Button under Accessibility. To choose a speed, go to the Speed menu.

Accessibility > Side Button may also be accessed via the Apple Watch app on the iPhone by tapping My Watch > Accessibility. The fastest option is to click here.

Make Physical Adaptations

1. Launch the Apple Watch's Settings menu.
2. To make any of the following changes, choose Accessibility > Touch Accommodations.

- React to touches for a certain amount of time: To modify the length of the hold, activate the feature and use the plus and minus buttons.

Swipe Gestures may be activated by tapping the option, and then Swipe Gestures can be used without the required hold time. You have the option of customizing the minimum distance a swipe motion needs to initiate.

- To disregard touches that occur too quickly after one another, activate Ignore Repeat and use the plus and minus buttons to choose the interval. After that, many rapid touches are interpreted by your Apple Watch as a single touch.
- Give an answer based on your first or last point of contact: You may choose to use the last touch location or the first.

When you tap an app from the Home Screen, for instance, your Apple Watch will utilize the point where you initially touched the screen. When you lift your finger from the display, your watch will detect a tap if you have Use Final Touch Location selected. When you tap Apple Watch, it will reply when you raise your finger. Use the plus and minus buttons to move the time around. If you wait longer than the gesture delay, your device will react to additional movements, such as drags.

Accessibility > Touch Accommodations may also be accessed via the Apple Watch app on the iPhone by selecting My Watch > Accessibility > Accessibility.

THE WATCH RTT ARRANGEMENT & USAGE

The RTT protocol is designed to communicate both text and sound in real-time. Apple Watch with cellular allows those with hearing or speech impairments to use RTT to communicate when apart from their iPhone. Apple Watch's Software RTT may be customized using the Apple Watch app and does not need any other hardware.

Not all carriers and areas enable RTT. In the United States, Apple Watch will use special characters or tones when placing an emergency call. The operator's reception and response to these tones may be affected by your physical location. Apple makes no promises about the operator's ability to accept or reply to an RTT call.

Activate The Real-Time Telemetry

1. Get out your iPhone and launch the Apple Watch app.
2. To activate RTT, tap My Watch, then choose Accessibility > RTT.
3. Select "Relay Number," and then type in the phone number you want to use for RTT relay calls.

4. Switch to the Sending Mode As you write, the characters will be sent out at once. Do not wait for all messages to be completed before sending.

Get An RTT Call Going

1. Launch the Apple Watch's Phone app.
2. Select Contacts with the Digital Crown, and then use the scroll wheel to browse.
3. Select the desired caller by tapping them, scrolling down, and finally tapping the RTT button.
4. Write a note, choose a prewritten response, or use an emoji to communicate.

Scribble is currently only accessible in English.

The Apple Watch displays the text similarly to an exchange of Messages.

If the other party in the call does not have RTT enabled, you will be informed.

Get On The RTT Call

1. Raise your wrist when you hear or feel a call alert to see who is calling.
2. Click the RTT button once you've scrolled down from the Answer button.
3. Write a note, choose a prewritten response, or use an emoji to communicate.

Scribble is currently only accessible in English.

Modify Canned Responses

You may quickly respond with a tap while making or receiving RTT calls on Apple Watch. Here's how you can make your unique responses:

1. Get out your iPhone and launch the Apple Watch app.
2. Select Default Replies by tapping My Watch, then Accessibility > RTT.
3. Simply touch "Add reply," type in your response, then hit "Done" when you're through.

   The standard form for ending a reply is "GA," which stands for "go ahead" and indicates to the recipient that they may continue with their reply.

When seeing your default responses, press Edit to make any necessary changes, remove responses, or rearrange their order.

ADJUSTING WATCH'S ACCESSIBILITY SETTINGS

Adjusting Watch's Accessibility Settings for Audio

Turn on Mono Audio to hear a merged left-and-right signal via the speakers or headphones attached to your Apple Watch. You may also change the left/right balance of stereo or mono audio on your Apple Watch. Accessibility settings are also modifiable on the AirPods.

Modify The Mono Volume And The Balance
To adjust your Apple Watch's hearing features, open the Settings app, choose Accessibility, and then select Hearing.

- Transform your sound from stereo to mono by selecting Mono Audio.
- Modify the volume level by choosing between Left and Right under Mono Audio.

To enable Mono Audio and tweak the volume, open the Apple Watch app on your iPhone, go to My Watch, and choose Accessibility.

Adapt Your Air Pods' Parameters
When paired with an Apple Watch, AirPods allow you to customize press speed and press-and-hold length. When using one AirPod in one ear, you may activate noise cancellation on AirPods Pro.

1. Launch the Apple Watch's Settings menu.
2. To adjust your AirPods' accessibility features, go to Settings > Accessibility > AirPods.

The Apple Watch app on the iPhone may also be accessed by going to My Watch > Accessibility > AirPods.

Play Back The Home Pod Transcripts

If you use the same Apple ID on your HomePod and Apple Watch, your Apple Watch will display text versions of any announcements made by your HomePod.

1. Launch the Apple Watch's Settings menu.
2. Click the Settings cog, and then choose Show Audio Transcriptions under Accessibility.

THE WATCH ACCESSIBILITY SHORTCUT

You may program a triple-click on the Digital Crown to activate or deactivate the following accessibility options: Helpful accessibility features such as AssistiveTouch, Control Nearby Devices, Left/Right Balance, Reduce Motion, Reduce Transparency, Touch Accommodations, VoiceOver, and Zoom may be activated.

Make A Shortcut Easily Reachable

1. Launch the Apple Watch's Settings menu.
2. Select one or more shortcuts under the Accessibility menu.

You can also access these settings from your iPhone by opening the Apple Watch app, selecting My Watch, then tapping Accessibility > Accessibility Shortcut.

Take The Easy Way Out

1. In a rapid sequence of three, press the Digital Crown.

   If you've programmed the shortcut to activate several features, choose the ones you want to use, and then press the Done button.

2. To disable the accessibility menu once again, triple-click the Digital Crown.

Reboot your Watch

If your Apple Watch and iPhone aren't functioning properly, you might try rebooting them.

Reboot your Watch

- Close the Apple Watch's lid: The Power Off slider may be moved to the right by pressing and holding the side button until the sliders show, then tapping the Power Button.
- To activate your Apple Watch, press and hold the side button until you see the Apple logo.

Digital Crown

Side button

Apple Watch's face with the Digital Crown and side button is prominently shown on the right side of the device.

The Apple Watch cannot be restarted while it is charging.

Sync Your iPhone By Rebooting

- To power down your iPhone, press and hold the side button and a volume button, and then move the power switch to the right if you have a Face ID model. A slider will appear; for devices without Face ID, press and hold the top or side button until it does. Settings > General > Shut Down is likewise available on all models.
- To activate your iPhone, press and hold either the side button or the top button until you see the Apple logo.

Restart Your Watch By Hand

If you are unable to power down your Apple Watch or the issue persists, you may need to do a hard reset. Only try this if restarting your Apple Watch has failed.

Forcing a restart requires simultaneously depressing the side button and the Digital Crown until the Apple logo shows, which should take at least 10 seconds.

Get Rid Of Watch

It may be necessary to factory reset your Apple Watch in some circumstances, such as if you have forgotten your password.

Clear Apple Watch data and preferences

1. Launch the Apple Watch's Settings menu.
2. Select Erase All Content and Settings by going to General > Reset and entering your PIN.

   You can either erase everything on your Apple Watch or cancel your cellular plan, or you may erase everything and keep your plan. Select Erase All to permanently delete all data from your Apple Watch. Select Erase All & Keep Plan if you need to delete everything but wish to keep your current mobile phone plan.

Alternatively, you may access the Apple Watch app on your iPhone, choose My Watch, go to General > Reset, and finally select Erase Apple Watch Content and Settings.

If you've forgotten your Apple Watch's passcode but still need to change certain settings, you may do it by charging the device, then pressing and holding the side button until the sliders show in the Settings app. Reset the device by pressing and holding the Digital Crown.

Activation Lock will be turned on when an Apple Watch is erased in this manner. If you lose or have your Apple Watch stolen, you can keep it secure from unauthorized use with the help of Activation Lock.

Once the reset is complete and the Apple Watch has restarted, you will need to re-pair it with your iPhone by launching the Apple Watch app on your iPhone and then following the on-screen prompts.

Cancel Your Mobile Phone Service
The cellular plan for an Apple Watch may be canceled at any time.

1. Get out your iPhone and launch the Apple Watch app.

2. Select Cellular from the My Watch screen, and then press the Info button that appears next to your cellular plan.
3. Select the carrier from the list, and then tap Remove Plan.

If you no longer want to include this Apple Watch in your monthly plan, you may need to contact your cellular provider.

Get Back Your Watch

If an animation of a watch and iPhone being moved closer together appears on your Apple Watch, try these steps:

1. The Apple Watch works best when the iPhone is close by.
   You'll need iOS 15.4 or later, an active internet connection, Bluetooth enabled, and an unlocked iPhone.
2. Charge your Apple Watch now.
3. To begin, double-click the Apple Watch's side button, and then adhere to the instructions shown on your iPhone.

BACK UP YOUR WATCH

Back up your Apple Watch, and then restore it.

When you connect your Apple Watch to an iPhone, the two devices will automatically back each other up. When you back up your iPhone to iCloud or a local Mac or PC, it also backs up your Apple Watch. You can't access the data in your iCloud backups unless you delete them first.

Watch May Be Backed Up And Restored

- Save a copy of your Apple Watch: When an Apple Watch is linked with an iPhone; the data on both devices is automatically backed up to the phone. Before you can unpair your devices, however, a backup must be made.
- If you lose your Apple Watch and later find it, or buy a new one, you may restore it from a previous backup by selecting "Restore from Backup" on your iPhone and then choosing the backup you want to use.

When a family member's Apple Watch is charged and connected to Wi-Fi, it will automatically back up to that person's iCloud account. Open the Settings app on the managed Apple Watch, go to [account name] > iCloud > iCloud Backups, and toggle the setting to "off."

Watch Software Update

The Apple Watch app on the iPhone may be used to check for software upgrades for the Apple Watch.

Update your software regularly
Be sure to update your software regularly.

1. Get out your iPhone and launch the Apple Watch app.
2. If an update is available, touch My Watch, then General, then Software Update, and finally Download and Install.

Alternatively, you may access Software Update from the General menu in the Settings app on your Apple Watch.

CHECK OUT WATCH'S PORTRAIT GALLERY

The Apple Watch app's Face Gallery provides quick access to all of the available watch faces. If you like the appearance of one in the gallery, you may modify it, add complexities, and save it to your collection all in one go.

The Portrait Gallery Is Opening

Launch the Apple Watch app on your iPhone, and then choose Face Gallery from the options at the app's bottom.

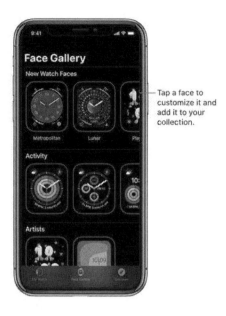

Tap a face to customize it and add it to your collection.

The Face Gallery in the Apple Watch app was activated. Watch faces are organized into many categories, such as "Activity" and "Artist," with "New" faces appearing in the top row. You may scroll down to see further face groups.

Pick Out Facial Characteristics

Select a face by tapping it in the Face Gallery, and then select a trait to modify it with.

The main display adapts as you experiment with various settings, allowing you to fine-tune the look.

The Face Gallery needs some more complexities.

1. To add a complication, choose it from the Face Gallery's list and then press Top Left, Top Right, or Bottom.
2. To choose a certain complication for that role, just swipe to see the options.
3. If you change your mind and decide you don't want the added complexity, just press Off at the very top of the list.

To give it a face

1. Tap Add after you're finished editing a face in the Face Gallery.
2. Swipe your finger over the Apple Watch face from left to right to get the new face.

CREATE YOUR WATCH FACE

Modify the Apple Watch face's appearance and features to suit your preferences. Pick a template, modify the colors and options, and add it to your archive. You may always change your appearance to get a different perspective on the clocks and other timekeeping devices.

The Apple Watch app's Face Gallery is the quickest and simplest method to browse watch faces, modify and save your own. Anyway, if you don't have your iPhone with you, you may change the face of your watch in any way you choose.

Swap Out The Watch's Face If You'd Like

- You may switch watch faces by swiping the screen from left to right.
- Touch and hold the watch face you want to view all of the possible watch faces, and then swipe to the one you want and press it to choose it.

Swipe left or right to see other watch faces.

Simple

Add features to your watch face.

The current watch face, together with Share and Edit buttons, is shown when you touch and hold the watch face. At midnight, the watch face title appears. Alternate watch faces may be seen by swiping left or right. Select a difficulty to tailor its characteristics to your needs.

Embellish The Watch Face With Extra Features

Some watch faces allow you to add extra features, or complexities, so that you may see information from other applications or check the stock market at a glance.

1. Touch and hold the screen while the watch face is shown, and then choose Edit.
2. To get to the end, swipe to the left.

   The complexities of a face are shown on the final screen if it has any.

3. Select a complication (such as Activity or Heart Rate) with a tap, then switch to a different one with a turn of the Digital Crown.
4. After making your adjustments, you may save them by pressing the Digital Crown, and then you can choose a different face by tapping it.

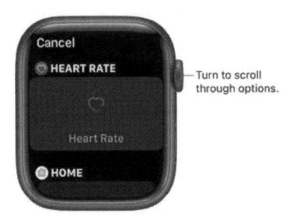

Turn to scroll through options.

The Heart Rate complication is featured on the watch face customization screen. Navigate the menu of difficulties by rotating the Digital Crown.

Complications are a common feature of certain App Store downloads.

Put A New Face On Your Watch

Make your unique font faces or several versions of the same design.

1. Touch and hold the screen while the current watch face is active.
2. To create a new list, swipe left until the list is empty, then press the plus sign (+).
3. Select a watch face by rotating the Digital Crown and tapping the Add button.

If you want to look at only the new watch faces in watchOS, you can do so by tapping the New collection.

Once it's been added, the watch face may be personalized.

Tap new, scroll to browse watch faces, then tap a face to add it.

An additional button has been added to the new watch face interface. Change the watch's face with a tap.

Check out what you've got
All of your watches' faces are seen.

1. Get out your iPhone and launch the Apple Watch app.
2. Select your watch face library by tapping My Watch and swiping underneath My Faces.

Select Edit, and then move the Reorder icon to the top or bottom next to the watch face you want to move.

Get Rid Of One Of Those Faces

1. Touch and hold the screen while the current watch face is active.
2. Simply touch the unwanted face, slide it up, and then hit Remove to get rid of it.

Or, you may use the Apple Watch software on your iPhone, go to the My Watch tab, and then edit your faces by tapping the Edit button. Select the watch faces you want to remove by tapping the Delete button next to them, then selecting Remove.

The watch face may be re-added at any time.

After swiping to a watch face and then swiping up on it to erase it, this screen appears on the Apple Watch.

Time Must Be Advanced

1. Launch the Apple Watch's Settings menu.
2. Use the Tap Clock.

3. To advance the time by up to 59 minutes, tap +0 min and then crank the Digital Crown.

This option only affects the watch face time, not the alarm or notification timings or any other time-based features (like World Clock).

FACETIME BETWEEN WATCHES

Faces for watches may be transferred between users. Both native watchOS complications and third-party complications may be used on shared faces.

The receiver must likewise have an Apple Watch running watchOS 7 or later to use the watch face.

Swap Watch Dials

1. Display the watch face you'd want to share from your Apple Watch.
2. To share content, touch and hold the screen before selecting the option.
3. Choose "Don't include" next to the complication you don't want to show off by tapping on the watch face's name.
4. Select a contact or select Messages/Mail.
   Select Messages or Mail, and then compose a new message with a contact, topic (Mail), and body.
5. Just hit the send button.

A watch face-sharing message appears on the Apple Watch display, along with the recipient's name. The "Add Contact" button and the name of the watch face are shown below, along with the recommendation to "Check out this watch face."

If you want to share a watch face from your collection or the Face Gallery, launch the Apple Watch app, choose the face, and then press the Share icon.

Obtain A Watch Dial

Shared watch faces may be obtained by web links, Messages, or Mail.

1. Check out a website, email, or text message that describes a shared watch face.
2. Add the watch face after tapping the shared watch face.

If a watch face with complexity is sent to you from an external app, you may open the App Store and download the app by tapping the price of the app or Get. If you'd like to use the watch face without the external widget, just press the Continue without This App button.

CHAPTER NINE

APPLE'S FITNESS APP ON YOUR WATCH

Apple Fitness+ subscribers get access to a variety of exercises and routines, including high-intensity interval training (HIIT), yoga, core training, cycling, strength training, treadmill workouts (running and walking), and dance. Metrics like heart rate and calories burnt are sent from your Apple Watch during exercise and sync with your daily activity data after you've finished your workout on your iPhone, iPad, or Apple TV.

Apple Fitness+ may be used without an Apple Watch if you're running iOS 16.1 or later. To choose a workout, launch the Fitness app on an iPhone 9 or later running iOS 16.1 or later, then hit Fitness+.

If you don't have an Apple Watch, you won't see your heart rate or calorie burn during workouts.

Guided meditations are also available to aid in the enhancement of one's general feeling of well-being.

You'll need an iPhone 6s or later running iOS 14.3 or later to get started with Apple Fitness+ on your Apple Watch Series 3. Use Apple Fitness+ on your iPad running iPadOS 14.3 or later, or on your Apple TV 4K or Apple TV HD running tvOS 14.3 to track your exercises alongside your compatible Apple Watch and iPhone.

Using Apple Fitness+ with an iPhone 9 or later running iOS 16, an iPad running iPadOS 16, and an Apple TV 4K or Apple TV HD running tvOS 16 will give you access to all of the latest features.

Apple Fitness+ is now only accessible in certain markets.

Select A Physical Activity

There are several possibilities available when it comes to physical activity. Details such as the playlist and music type closed captioning availability, and the need for equipment like dumbbells or a mat (most exercises do not require equipment) are shown for each activity to assist you make your selection. The exercise routine may be previewed as well.

Locate a Teacher

The Fitness+ homepage includes featured routines, a weekly exercise video, and workout recommendations.

Apple Fitness+ trainers are all individuals who add their sense of style and flair to the exercises they lead. In the Fitness app, you can learn about each trainer and access a complete catalog of exercises designed by each instructor.

Examine Your Data

Keep score of how far you've gotten in each ring throughout your exercise. In addition to monitoring your heart rate and calorie burn on your Apple Watch, you can do so on your iOS device or Apple TV while you're out.

Fitness+ routines on watchOS 9 provide both trainer assistance and on-screen instructions to maximize your results. Intensity, strokes per minute (SPM), revolutions per minute (RPM), and incline are all shown on the screen for high-intensity interval training, cycling, rowing, and treadmill users.

The Burn Bar is a feature available during cycling, HIIT, rowing, and treadmill workouts that compares your performance stats to those of other users. The higher up on the Burn Bar you are, the more calories you have burned. The workout summary stores your Burn Bar ranking among the other data you've tracked throughout the session.

JOIN APPLE'S FITNESS+ PROGRAM

With an Apple One Premier membership, you may save money by bundling Apple Fitness+ with other Apple services.

Not all locations or countries support Apple Fitness+ or Apple One Premier.

Download the Fitness App

You'll need the Fitness app on your iPhone, iPad, or Apple TV to utilize Apple Fitness+. You may get the

Fitness app from the App Store if it isn't already installed on your iOS device.

Join Apple's Fitness+ Program

1. Launch Fitness on your Apple device (iPhone/iPad/Apple TV). The next step is to open Fitness+ on your iPhone.
2. To start your free trial, click the button and then follow the on-screen prompts to enter your Apple ID and confirm your membership.

Put an end to your Apple Fitness+ membership.

1. Choose one of these actions:
   - Launch the Fitness app and, if using an iPhone, choose Summary. To access Apple Fitness+, hit your profile image, then [account name].
   - To add Apple Fitness+ to your Apple TV, launch the Settings app and go to Users and Accounts > [account name] > Subscriptions.
2. To modify or terminate your membership, please adhere to the on-screen prompts.

Family Sharing With Apple's Fitness
Family Sharing allows you to give several people access to Apple's fitness app.

Family Sharing allows you to share your Apple Fitness+ or Apple One Premier membership with up to five family members. If you have an Apple Watch Series 3 or later, your family members will automatically have access to Apple Fitness+ the next time they open the Fitness app after your membership starts. Apple Fitness+ may be used with an Apple TV or an iPad if a family member has an Apple Watch but no iPhone (since their Apple Watch was set up by a family member).

Removing a family member from a Family Sharing group will end their access to your Apple Fitness+ membership.

PREPARE APPLE TV FOR APPLE FITNESS+

A TV displays the Apple Fitness+ interface with several exercise options and a suggested cycling routine.

You can use Apple Fitness+ anywhere you go thanks to the compatibility between your Apple Watch and the Fitness app on Apple TV 4K or Apple TV HD running tvOS 14.3 or later.

Join Your Apple TV And Watch Together
Apple Fitness+ requires an Apple Watch connection to Apple TV.

1. Launch the Apple TV's Fitness app.
2. Click on your name or "Other if it isn't listed.

   If you haven't already done so, you may need to choose Sign In from the Fitness app's menu on your Apple TV.

3. Select the Link from your Apple Watch.

   You may have to launch the Apple Watch's Workout app before you can press Connect.

4. If asked, choose Continue, and then input the code shown on your Apple TV into your Apple Watch.

Apple TV workouts need watchOS 7.2 or later, an unlocked Apple Watch, and Bluetooth switched on.

Pick Your Gym Buddies

With Apple TV's Fitness app, switching between family members is a breeze thanks to the Family Sharing feature. Apple Fitness+ users who aren't part of your Family Sharing group may use your Apple TV to work out with you.

1. Launch the Apple TV's Fitness app.
2. Click on your name or "Other if it isn't listed.

   Select Sign In in the Fitness app on your Apple TV if you haven't already done so.

3. If you'd like to share your Fitness app with a friend or family member, just tap the profile symbol in the upper left corner, and then tap Sign out.

EXPLORE THE APPLE FITNESS+ LIBRARY

Explore the Apple Fitness+ library for a variety of exercises and relaxation techniques.

Whether you're looking for a workout, a meditation, or a regimen, Apple Fitness+ has you covered. You may choose an exercise depending on your activity level, or you can sort and filter workouts of a certain category, or you can search for individual workouts or meditations. All other kinds of exercises begin at ten minutes, the Mindful Cooldown workouts begin at five, and there are always brand new Mindful Cooldown workouts introduced each week. Five, 10, or twenty minutes is an appropriate time for meditation.

Exercises And Obtain Suggestions
You may look through exercises and obtain suggestions.

Exercise routines from Fitness+ are organized into "More of What You Do" and "Try Something New" on an iPad.

Apple Fitness+ makes exercise suggestions based on your previous activity in the Workout app for Apple Watch and other compatible applications. If you want to add variety to your training regimen, Apple

Fitness+ will recommend different trainers and exercises.

1. Launch Fitness on your Apple device (iPhone/iPad/Apple TV). The next step is to open Fitness+ on your iPhone.
2. Research exercises and instructors:
   - Sort Exercises by Type You may check out the many exercise options up there by scrolling left and right.
   - Select audio exercises to play on your Apple Watch from apps like Time to Walk and Time to Run (iPhone only).

     Time to Walk or Time to Run episodes may be added to Apple Watch by tapping the Add button. Open the exercise app on your Apple Watch, choose Audio Workouts, scroll down, select Library, and then select the exercise to listen to. Scroll down, choose Time to Walk or Time to Run, and then rotate the Digital Crown to see further episodes.

     With iOS 16, you may now listen to episodes of Time to Walk and Time to Run on your iPhone.

   - View prominent exercise routines by selecting a subheading, such as Recently Added,

Recently Updated, Beginner, Popular, Simple, or Quick.

- You may filter trainer exercises by kind, duration, and music genre by scrolling down to the trainer row and then selecting a trainer from the left or right side of the screen.

  You may see all available trainers on an iOS device by selecting Show All.

- More of What You Already Do: Search for Apple Watch and third-party fitness app routines that are similar to the ones you've already completed, or that include the same coaches.
- Do Something Different: Discover other versions of your current regimen with new trainers and exercises to keep things interesting.
- Workouts are added to My Library through the Workout Details or Workout Summaries page (only available on iOS devices). You may utilize My Library to bookmark your favorite exercises, create a regimen, and even play workouts offline.

Browse & get started with meditations

1. Launch Fitness on your Apple device (iPhone/iPad/Apple TV). The next step is to open Fitness+ on your iPhone.
2. Select "Meditation" from the menu bar.
3. Choose one of these actions:
   - To start a meditation session, choose it from the menu and then hit Let's Begin.
   - Select a trainer, time, and topic using the Filter button, select a session with the Session button, and start with the Let's Begin button.

Your heart rate and the amount of time that has passed during the meditation are shown on your Apple Watch. To stop, continue, or quit the meditation, swipe right.

While the meditation is playing in the background, you may begin your exercise by tapping the exercise button. To access playback options reminiscent of Apple's Music app, swipe left.

If you have an Apple Fitness+ subscription, the Mindfulness app on your Apple Watch will allow you to listen to guided meditations.

Consider using an exercise or meditation series.

1. Launch Fitness on your Apple device (iPhone/iPad/Apple TV). The next step is to open Fitness+ on your iPhone.

2. Pick a system.

   The amount of workouts in a certain program is shown on each program tile.

3. To take any action:
   - A Sneak Peek at the Show: Tap View the Film to learn more about the program's aims and the exercises you may expect to complete. Reading about the program is another option for getting information.
   - Simply press the Add button next to the episode you'd want to add, or the Add All option if you'd like to add all episodes to My Workouts.
   - Get the show started with an episode: Choose an episode from the available options, and then hit the play button to start the exercise.

Next Workout will automatically show the next episode when you finish an episode to assist you retain your position, but you are free to choose any episode at any moment.

Classify physical activities

An iPad displaying the Yoga exercise filtering options available in Fitness+.

Sort and filter particular sorts of exercises (such as Rowing or Dance) by a trainer, duration of the workout, music genre, and more to discover the activity you're searching for.

1. Launch Fitness on your Apple device (iPhone/iPad/Apple TV). The next step is to open Fitness+ on your iPhone.
2. Choose a form of exercise from the options below.
   - Classify Exercises: Select sorting criteria, such as Trainer or Time, by tapping Sort.
   - Filter conditioning: Select the desired filter(s) by tapping Filter.

There are no relevant exercises for the selected filter.

Workouts that you have completed previously will get a checkmark next to their thumbnails while you are browsing.

GET YOUR FITNESS+ ROUTINE STARTED

Apple Fitness+ routines are accessible via your iOS device or Apple TV. The Apple Fitness+ routines are designed to be challenging regardless of your fitness level, so you can use them whether you're just starting or are a seasoned pro. After beginning an exercise, you have the option to stop, restart, and afterward evaluate the session.

Get Moving With Your iOS Device

1. Release the Fitness program. The next step is to open Fitness+ on your iPhone.
   You may get the Fitness app from the App Store if it isn't already installed on your iOS device.
2. Select an exercise category (such as Popular or Guest Trainer Series) or a specific workout from the menu at the top of the screen.
3. To take any action:
   - Insert the exercise into My Workouts: Just hit the "Add Workout" button.

- To see an example of the exercise routine before you start, just tap the Preview button.

The workout's accompanying music is also viewable. If you have a paid Apple Music subscription, you may access the playlist thereby selecting Listen in Music.

- To begin the exercise, launch the app on your iPhone, iPad, or Apple Watch, and hit the button that initiates the program, followed by the Play button. To get the most out of your Treadmill exercise, decide whether you want to run or walk before you begin.

You may begin the exercise even if you're not wearing an Apple Watch, but no data will be recorded from it. To begin your exercise, choose Work Out without Watch from the menu.

During a workout, you may press the screen, hit the AirPlay button, and then pick a destination, such as a TV or HomePod, that supports AirPlay 2.0.

Apple TV may also be used to kick off an exercise routine. Learn more about the assignment by reading on.

Extra trainers show you how to modify the exercises to make them easier or harder, depending on your fitness level. Exercise modifications, such as doing a dumbbell exercise using just one's body weight, may also be suggested by trainers.

Get Moving With An Apple TV Exercise

1. Select the exercisers from the Fitness app.
2. Choose a category of exercise, then a specific routine, to get started.
3. To take any action:
   - A look forward at the routine: Choose Preview.
   - Kick off your exercise by: If you haven't already joined, start your free trial now, otherwise start your exercise.

     To get the most out of your Treadmill exercise, decide whether you want to run or walk before you begin.

   - Listen to the workout's featured tunes in Music: Select a song from the list to play on the Music app (an Apple Music membership is needed).
   - You can check out the other exercises in the category by scrolling down to the Related Workouts row and then clicking the left or right arrows.

Take A Break From Your Training
You may take a break from your training and come back to it later.

Either the device playing the exercise or your Apple Watch may be used to pause it.

- If you have an Apple Watch, you can:
  - ❖ To temporarily halt a workout, press the side button and Digital Crown simultaneously. You may also hit the Pause button and swipe left or right.
  - ❖ Pressing the side button and the Digital Crown together, swiping right and selecting Resume, or swiping left and selecting Play will resume an exercise routine.
- You can accomplish any of the following on an iOS device:
  - ❖ Exercise break: Select the Pause button by tapping the screen.
  - ❖ To go back to your exercise, just hit the Play button.
- On an Apple TV:
  - ❖ Workout breaks and restarts: To activate Siri, either press the middle of the click pad (Siri Remote 2) or the touch surface (Siri Remote 1). To begin, use the Play/Pause button on the Siri Remote.

Summing Up A Workout

Either the device playing the exercise or your Apple Watch may be used to stop the session early.

- To dismiss a notification on Apple Watch, swipe right.
  Your workout stats will be shown. A return to the Workout app is only a tap away.
- To terminate a workout on an iOS device, choose End, then End Workout.

  Your workout stats will be shown. To save the routine to My Workouts, use the Add button; to share it; to select a cooldown routine from Mindful Cooldown; or to exit back to Apple Fitness+, select Done.

- To end a workout on Apple TV, go to the Menu screen by pressing the Siri Remote or Apple TV Remote's Menu button.

  Your workout stats will be shown. To pick a cooldown exercise or to go back to Apple Fitness+, click the Mindful Cooldown option.

The iPhone's Fitness app stores your exercise data so you may review it at a later time.

A class that you have already attended will have a checkmark next to its thumbnail in the list of exercises.

WORKOUT TOGETHER WITH THE SHARE PLAY

You and up to 32 of your closest friends may get in a workout together with the help of SharePlay Group Workouts. Initiate a FaceTime conversation on your iOS device, and then go to the Fitness app on your iOS device or Apple TV to begin a Group Workout.

Whether you're doing high-intensity interval training (HIIT), cardio-intensive cycling (Circuit Training), or low-impact aerobics (Rowing), the workout will play in sync with all participants and can be controlled from individual devices.

For Apple Fitness+ Group Workouts, you'll need one of the following Apple products: Devices running iOS 15.1 or later are supported, including the iPhone, iPad, and iPod touch. tvOS 15.1 or later is required for playback on Apple TV. Macs need to be running macOS Monterey 12.1, or later, for playback. Not all nations or areas have access to FaceTime or all of FaceTime's functionality. This also holds for other Apple services. Apple Watch

Series 4 or later running watchOS 9.1 or later is required for usage during exercise.

Group workouts may be kicked off on an iPhone or iPad via FaceTime.

1. Initiate a call with FaceTime.
2. Start up the Fitness app on your Apple device. The next step is to open Fitness+ on your iPhone.
3. The Fitness app is available in the App Store if you don't already have it.

   Choose a routine, launch it, and then hit SharePlay to get everyone on the call moving at the same time. (Others on the call may need to choose Open when requested to utilize SharePlay to take part in the Group Workout.)

   The exercise playlist begins playing simultaneously for all listeners on the call. Those without access are encouraged to get it (through a subscription or free trial if offered).

The exercise may be played and paused using the devices' (including Apple Watches') native playback controls.

You may cancel an exercise at any time by tapping the X in the upper left corner of the screen on your iPhone or iPad. Swipe right to dismiss a notification on your Apple Watch.

Start A Group Workout

1. Launch the Fitness app on your iOS device, then choose "Group Workout."
2. Start up the Fitness app on your Apple device. The next step is to open Fitness+ on your iPhone.
3. The Fitness app is available in the App Store if you don't already have it.
4. Just choose a workout, hit "More," then "SharePlay" to broadcast it.

Select FaceTime and add the people you want to work out with to the To box.

Select Let's Begin after the FaceTime call has connected.

To join in on the exercise, the receiver should hit the workout's title at the top of the FaceTime interface, then press Open. The exercise playlist begins playing simultaneously for all listeners on the call. Those without access are encouraged to get it (through a subscription or free trial if offered).

The exercise may be played and paused using the devices' (including Apple Watches') native playback controls.

You may cancel an exercise at any time by tapping the X in the upper left corner of the screen on your iPhone or iPad. Swipe right to dismiss a notification on your Apple Watch.

Train With Others Using Apple TV

SharePlay on Apple TV allows you to participate in a Group Workout.

The SharePlay buttons won't show up until the same Apple ID is used on both the Apple TV and the iOS device being used for the FaceTime call. Pressing and holding the TV button on the Siri Remote will bring up Apple TV's Control Center, where you may choose a new user or create a new one.

1. Make a FaceTime call using an iOS device.

   When a FaceTime call is active, Apple TV will recognize it and an indication for SharePlay will display in the top right corner of the Home Screen.

2. Launch the Fitness app by doing one of the following on your Apple TV:

- Get your exercise going, then when asked on your iOS device, choose SharePlay and confirm.
- To do this, open Control Center on your iOS device by pressing and holding the TV button on the Siri Remote, then tap the SharePlay button, tap Join, and finally tap Confirm on your iOS device.
3. Go ahead and choose an exercise from Fitness if you haven't already.

All of the devices participating in the FaceTime session, including Apple TV, will play the exercise at the same time. Everyone can control playback in real-time using the controls on their own devices.

MODIFY THE DISPLAYED STATISTICS

Alter the visuals in Apple Fitness+ programs like meditation and workouts.

During your routine, your smartphone will provide real-time data on how far along you are in each ring. Wearing an Apple Watch while exercising is a great way to keep tabs on your heart rate and calorie expenditure.

Time, heart rate, and calorie burn data are shown on the screen during an Apple Fitness+ core exercise.

The Burn Bar is an additional feature of certain exercises that displays how your stats stack up to those of previous users of the same activity. The higher up on the Burn Bar you are, the more calories you have burned. The workout summary stores your Burn Bar ranking among the other data you've tracked throughout the session.

During a workout, you may customize the Apple Watch stats that are shown on the screen. The Fitness app's metrics are synchronized across all of your Apple ID-enabled devices.

Apple Watch users who subscribe to Fitness+ and have an AirPlay-enabled display may now view real-time personal analytics throughout their exercises.

1. Select the Metrics option while you're working out.

   Here are some motions to utilize when working out with Apple TV:

   - To access the Metrics pane on the second-generation Siri Remote, press down on the click pad ring or slide down on the click pad.
   - To access the Metrics pane on the first-generation Siri Remote, swipe down to see the Info pane.
2. Choose one of these actions:
   - Disable all analytics by clicking the Show Analytics toggle.
     All of your metrics are still being tracked, but you won't be able to see them.
   - Select "Off," "Show Time Elapsed," or "Show Time Remaining" to alter the time display.

     Reducing power Time is still shown on the interval timer.

   - The Burn Bar should be turned off, so just does that.

     Turning off the Burn Bar prevents your workouts from adding to the community burn bar and prevents you from seeing your position after a session.

Put On The Closed Captions And Subs

Standard captions and subtitles for the deaf and hard of hearing (SDH) are available for all Apple Fitness+ exercises and meditations. Below the workout's duration, genre, and addition date, you'll notice whether closed captioning and SDH are available.

- To change the language during a workout on an iPhone or iPad, press the More icon, then select Subtitles.
- to get the most out of your Apple TV exercise, you may either:
  - ❖ For the second-generation Siri Remote, choose a language by pressing down on the click pad ring or swiping down on the click pad to see the Info window.
  - ❖ With the original Siri Remote, you could choose subtitles in a different language by swiping down from the top of the touch screen to reveal the Info menu.

INDEX

Made in the USA
Monee, IL
02 April 2024

be3539a4-2f90-4b7e-ab40-9cecbe89a728R03